Is Peace Possible?

Is Peace Possible?

Introduced by
MARIA POPOVA

Kathleen Lonsdale

CANONGATE

This Canongate edition published in Great Britain in 2025 by Canongate Books Ltd.,
14 High Street, Edinburgh EH1 1TE

First published in Great Britain in 1957
by Penguin Books

canongate.co.uk

1

British Library Cataloguing-in-Publication Data
A catalogue record for this book is available on
request from the British Library

ISBN 978 1 83726 421 6

Printed and bound by CPI Group (UK) Ltd, Croydon CR0 4YY

The manufacturer's authorised representative in the EU for product safety
is Authorised Rep Compliance Ltd, 71 Lower Baggot Street,
Dublin D02 P593 Ireland (arccompliance.com)

MIX
Paper | Supporting
responsible forestry
FSC® C013604

AUTHOR'S NOTE

When the news of the dropping of the first atomic bomb on Hiroshima appeared in the British newspapers, an actress friend of mine, not a pacifist, came to me in a fury and said, 'Do you see what you scientists have done now?' This is an attempt to answer that question. It is written in a personal way because I feel a sense of corporate guilt and responsibility that scientific knowledge should have been so misused. It includes an even more limited attempt to suggest what we, the scientists, and all those who desire a world in which our grandchildren can grow up happily, ought to be doing.

I am indebted to members of the Peace Committee of the Society of Friends (Quakers) who gave me the initial encouragement to write; and to many other Friends and friends of the Friends for written and verbal suggestions and criticisms, of which I have made extensive use.

FOREWORD

How ungenerous our culture has been in portraying science as cold, unfeeling, and aloof from the human sphere. No—to live a life of science is to live so wonder-smitten by reality, by the majesty and mystery of nature, that the willful destruction of any fragment of it becomes unconscionable. It is impossible to study the building blocks of life without reverence for life itself, impossible to devote one's days to the enigma of a single element or elementary particle without venerating the inviolable cohesion of the universe. There is a kind of innocent exhilaration to this sense of wonder, and a quiet ethic. It may well be our greatest antidote to self-destruction.

This exuberance drove Kathleen Lonsdale (1903–1971) to regularly run the last few yards to her laboratory, to puzzle over differential equations throughout her pregnancies and take her calculations into the maternity ward.

The tenth child in a Quaker household without electricity, she was born in Ireland the year the Wright brothers built and flew humanity's first successful flying machine heavier than air. Her home was still lit by gas when she first began studying science—in a school for boys, because no such subjects figured into the curriculum of the local girls' school. By the time she was a teenager, living outside London, she watched gas-filled zeppelins rain bombs and death from the air. She watched them plummet in flames, shot down by British weapons. She watched her mother cry with the knowledge that piloting them were German boys not much older than Kathleen.

After attaining a higher score in physics than any London University student ever had, she joined the Cambridge laboratory of J. D. Bernal–the first scientist to apply X-ray crystallography to the molecules of life. He came to see how beneath her quiet, unassuming manner lay "such an underlying strength of character that she became from the outset the presiding genius of the place."

Soon, she was pioneering uses of X-ray crystallography that would fuel the chemistry of the century to come: still in her twenties, Lonsdale illuminated the shape, dimensions, and atomic structure of the benzene ring that had mystified chemists since Michael Faraday discovered benzene a century earlier.

The first woman tenured at London's most venerated research university and the first female president of both the British Association for the Advancement of Science and the International Union of Crystallography, Lonsdale was also one of the twentieth century's most lucid, impassioned, and indefatigable activists against our civilizational cult of war and the military industrial complex's funding its planet-sized house of worship. By the time the next World War broke out, Lonsdale—by then one of the world's preeminent scientists—was imprisoned as a conscientious objector to military conscription. She went on to become one of Europe's most influential prison reformers, recognizing that the prison industrial complex is the price societies governed by the military industrial complex pay for the inequalities and injustices stemming from that foundational cult.

Lonsdale wrote *Is Peace Possible* in 1957 as part of a Penguin series that invited some of the era's most lucid and luminous minds to reckon with some of the era's most urgent questions. It is perspectival and prophetic. "History teaches us that time can bring about reconciliations that seemed at another time impossible, but only when violence has ceased, whether by agreement or through exhaustion," Lonsdale writes in the middle of the Cold War that never erupted into the nuclear holocaust it could have been, largely thanks to the Pugwash Conference for nuclear disarmament, in which she was involved and which reached agreements thought unimaginable. It is difficult today to imagine how real the doom felt to the children ducking under school desks, how improbable its aversion given the geopolitical forces at play—and yet here we are, survivors of an abated apocalypse, here to tell its story: the story of the triumph of the possible over the probable, the triumph of peace.

Bridging the spiritual ethos of her upbringing with the scientific worldview of her calling and training, Lonsdale challenges the misconception of pacifism as the simplistic idea that a perfect and peaceful world is merely a matter of individuals refusing to fight. "Truism based on Utopias are poor arguments," she observes, instead invoking the style of pacifism native to the Quaker tradition and its original formulation in 1660 as the refusal to partake of "all outward wars and strife, and fightings with outward weapons, for any end, or under any pretence whatever." Peace, she argues, is the product of the recognition "that war is spiritually degrading, that it is the wrong way to settle disputes between classes or nations, the wrong way to meet aggression or oppression, the wrong way to preserve national or personal ideals." It is wrong not merely in a philosophical sense but in a practical sense, for we are far too interdependent to harm another without harming ourselves. To illustrate the interleaving of lives across the artificial pickets of national borders, she looks back on the 1947 cholera epidemic that quickly came to claim five hundred lives per day in Egypt but was also quickly curbed after twenty nations cooperated on a supply line for vaccines. In a sentiment of staggering timeliness in the wake of the twenty-first century's deadliest pandemic, Lonsdale observes that "plagues are no respecters of sovereignty," nor are the far-reaching economic, moral, spiritual, and radioactive consequences of war.

Ultimately, Lonsdale indicts the underlying reason for the existence of war lurking beneath all surface conflicts: Military alliances and international treaties only gauze the open wound of widespread inequality and injustice that colonialism and capitalism have inflicted on our world. "Real security can only be found, if at all, in a world without the injustices that now exist, and without arms," she insists. At the heart of her slender masterwork of moral courage is a vision for how such a world might be possible:

"There are two ways in which such changes might come. One is the way of the compulsion of experience, the whip and spur of historical inevitability, the coercion of facts. That is the hard and bitter way. The other is the way of foresight, of preparation, of imagination. It is also the way of moral compulsion. It may be no less hard but it is not bitter."

Maria Popova
New York, 2025

I am a member of the Society of Friends, sometimes called Quakers, and I am a convinced pacifist, but I find it very hard to convince other people.

The Quaker form of pacifism which expresses itself in terms of the Declaration to Charles II, 1660, is usually respected, but is often found to be singularly irritating if it is offered as a recipe for the cure of all the evils of war. So is the statement

> We utterly deny all outward wars and strife, and fightings with outward weapons, for any end, or under any pretence whatever; this is our testimony to the whole world. The Spirit of Christ by which we are guided is not changeable, so as once to command us from a thing as evil, and again to move unto it; and we certainly know, and testify to the world, that the Spirit of Christ, which leads us into all truth, will never move us to fight and war against any man with outward weapons, neither for the kingdom of Christ, nor for the kingdoms of this world.

Wars would cease if men refused to fight.

It is true, of course. I have said it myself when discussing the place of personal pacifism in the creation of a world without war. But truisms based on Utopias are poor arguments.

The man or woman who is sure, whether through the guidance of the Spirit of Christ or the guidance of their reasoning powers or both, that war is spiritually degrading, that it is the wrong way to settle disputes between classes or nations, the wrong way to meet aggression or oppression, the wrong way to preserve national or personal ideals: that man or woman who is *sure* of this must obviously take no part in war and indeed must actively oppose it. Most civilized nations are beginning to realize that there is such a thing as a genuinely conscientious objection to personal participation in war, even if they do not regard it as expedient to encourage young people to think along these lines or to take this stand.

Curiously enough, even predominantly humanist or atheist communities seem to think that a conscience, if genuine, must be expressed in terms of religion. The young boy who feels that it is wrong to take any part in war, and justifies his refusal by arguing that war is contrary to common sense, is often, quite wrongly, rejected as a 'conscientious' objector. Yet humanism and communism both lay great stress on active benevolence towards one's fellow men. If God be denied, the well-being of humanity can still be regarded as desirable, at the lowest in terms of the survival of the race. Whether this is the manifestation of conscience, of instinct, or of reason I don't know, but it looks very much like a rationalization of conscience to me.

Most people, however, are not sure of anything. Certainly they are not sure either that they know God's will, or that anyone else does. They are not sure that it is wrong to fight, if by fighting one can alter intolerable conditions, or prevent large-scale communal crime, or get rid of a dangerous dictator before he gains too much power, or stand up to international blackmail, or ward off an armed attack. In terms of reason, they find it arguable – as it is – to say that although every possible way to avoid war must be sought, yet until men are perfect there will always be some who want to grab more than their share. They see no reason why this should be permitted if it can be prevented by the limited use of military force. They are pretty sure that it *is* prevented in many cases by the knowledge that force is there to stop it. For men are not perfect, but neither are they foolish enough, as a rule, to burgle or murder even on a national scale, if they know that they will be stopped and punished.

'The rule of law must prevail,' says Mr Selwyn Lloyd. 'We are not bellicose—neither the British Government nor the British people. With

Britain force is always the last resort.'[1] What this means we have seen in the Middle East. But, in any case, if force is to be the last resort, then military organization must exist, and its extent depends upon a political estimate of what international (or internal) problems it may be called upon to deal with.

National pacifism is something quite different from personal pacifism. It cannot come about until most people are convinced that it is not merely right but practicable to abandon military organization. To say that 'what is right *must* be practicable' presupposes a whole philosophy, or theology, that is by no means acceptable either to the majority of people or to those who have the immediate responsibility of making political decisions. Politicians have to consider all the possible repercussions of their actions. They don't always, of course; they often make what hindsight shows to have been the most elementary oversights. But then there are bad politicians as well as good. Let us confine ourselves to the good ones. Looking at all the possible courses of action, they are hardly to be blamed if they feel that the best among the practicable courses of action is the 'right' one in the given circumstances.

They don't usually mind having a few idealists around pressing fundamental principles. They are very tolerant of them. They give them interviews occasionally and may sometimes even pick up a useful phrase from what they say. It would be a poor look-out for the community if the only pressure groups were those with a material axe to grind. As a leading politician (not British) once said to me, 'Pacifism is not practical politics. But to be spiritually healthy every nation needs to have a spear-point of idealist opinion.' He meant it kindly. I am sure he believed what he said. But too often the idealist, in his anxiety to avoid appearing to be able to present a blueprint for the solution of any and every political problem, seems to imagine that he need never think in terms of real politics at all.

Certainly many, many people who are not pacifists think that it is not very much use their having political views or pressing them. They confine their

1 BBC Broadcast; 14 August 1956.

politics to the rare occasions on which they put a cross on a ballot paper. We do not, in this country, go in for plebiscites, and people are not therefore forced to make a personal decision on political matters. It certainly does very often seem as if unpopular policies, like the rearmament of Germany, are being forced through against the will of the majority of a bewildered but inarticulate British people, who wonder what on earth they fought for – twice.

There are quite a number of people who think that not only is this so, but that it should be so. I have been told quite seriously by university students (and it is certainly the opinion of many of their seniors) that having once voted, the ordinary citizen should expect to leave all political decisions to the successful members of Parliament and not concern himself with politics. It is not his business.

The pacifist who argues that he is concerned only with principles, and that politics are not his business, is usually evading the discipline and the responsibility of hard thinking. His position is a logical one only if he does not either expect or desire the politician to put pacifist principles into practise for him. He won't expect it, but if he does desire it then it is incumbent on him to study the world situation and try to decide for himself how it might be done, in general at least, if not in particular.

A very good case can be made out for the argument that the Christian should concentrate on his own and his neighbours' spiritual well-being and on his own personal behaviour; and that he should keep himself unspotted by the world of politics. That Christians, as such, should form an ideal community within the community; in it but not of it.

This would not be the position of most Friends, because they believe that religion should be part of all life, and our lives are intermingled. William Penn said, 'True Godliness doesn't turn men out of the world, but enables them to live better in it, and excites their endeavours to mend it.' It may well be that a community of Christians could, by showing their love for one another, show also what the larger community of the world might become, but the world is now small and to say that we are not responsible for our own Government's home or foreign policy is to say, in effect, 'Am I my brother's keeper?'

Nor does this imply that politicians in general have no principles and need to have them supplied. Of course they have them; but they also have a very heavy load of responsibility. It certainly seems as if they do sometimes find Christian principles impractical or conflicting, and which of us is fit to judge them for that? Are we ourselves without sin? Yet it was a terrible shock to many people when in September 1949, one week after declaring firmly that Britain would not go off the gold standard, the then Chancellor of the Exchequer, Sir Stafford Cripps, a man universally respected and even revered for the integrity and uprightness of his character, announced the devaluation of the pound sterling. To his critics he replied that if he had hinted at this in advance, or even refused to make any statement at all, there would have been wild speculation on the Stock Exchange.

This of course was true. It does not alter the fact that for many people truthfulness in politics has now become a mockery. A statesman has only to deny a rumour publicly for it to be regarded as reasonably certain that there is something in it. Anyone who listens to the radio in a mixed company of thinking people knows how deep-seated this cynicism is. It is only a little less tragic than the fact that many more people do believe what they hear on the radio or read in their newspapers, without giving the matter any further thought.

On the other hand it is simply not possible for the average citizen to know the detailed history of every political problem, to be able to savour the local feeling, to appreciate the legal situation, the probable reactions to and repercussions of particular courses of action. He has to rely on what he reads in the Press. A few newspaper editors seem to be able to comment intelligently, or at least fluently, on whatever is the current item of news, whether it be the nationalization of the Suez Canal, the latest revolution in Latin America, revolt in Hungary, border incidents in Burma, or recent research on the effect of fall-out from nuclear weapons. There is an occasional citizen who is knowledgeable about one of these; but if so, he is usually almost entirely ignorant about all the rest. An exceptionally unbiased person will read one newspaper of the right and another of the left and by balancing out their opinions, will feel free to form his own on the basis of their common facts, if any.

Of course it is always possible to ask questions, though not always to get the answer. When a politician says that a certain action on the part of some other Government is 'a breach of international law', he seldom quotes the law to which he refers. It is a good oratorical flourish, and as long as no-one can answer back, he sometimes gets away with it. He may be answered by a lawyer specializing in International Law, perhaps in a letter to *The Times*. It starts a correspondence, and makes entertaining reading. Many British people will go on thinking that we British are the upholders of world probity.

The tragic fact is, however, that a politician who loses his temper and makes offensive remarks is now heard by all the world: and because, unlike scientists – who have to calculate their 'probable error' – politicians (outside the communist countries, where we doubt their motives anyhow) seldom if ever admit having made a mistake, these remarks continue to rankle. You can forgive and even, in a way, admire a man who swindles you if he does it courteously, more easily than you can forgive the man who helps you but shows nevertheless that he dislikes or despises you. What intelligent Asians or Africans resent is not so much that we have enriched ourselves at their expense: they will often freely admit the benefits of British colonial administration, at its best: but what they resent is the fact that we have thought of and treated them as 'lesser breeds'. And this attitude on our part applies, I'm afraid, not only to Asians and Africans, but at times to anyone who is not British. Conscious superiority is not confined to the British, of course.

One effect of feeling conscious moral superiority is that we are apt to doubt the intelligence of those who do not agree with our moral judgements. If the British citizen and the British politician feel like this, it is often even more typical of the man or woman with a mission. The most salutary exercise possible, therefore, for a would-be reformer is to have to make the intellectual effort to understand the world situation and the people who are supposed to need reforming.

The remainder of this pamphlet represents such an effort. It is an attempt to see the 300-year-old Quaker peace testimony against the background of modern science, of modern politics, of modern men, and of future problems: to answer, if possible, the question 'Yes, that is all very well. World war has become suicidal, and little wars may grow into big ones. Nobody wants war and everyone wants their own way. So what?'

The one subject I do know something about is science. Let me begin with that. Is science friend or fiend? Forty years ago, when I began to study science at school, we had gas, but no electricity in our house. My brother worked in one of the first radio stations in the south-west of Ireland, but radio in the home was a thing of the future. Television was a fantastic dream. I had been born in the year in which the Wright brothers built and flew the first successful heavier-than-air machine, and six years later Bleriot had flown across the English Channel, but in 1916 the bombs that fell on our London suburb were dropped not from aeroplanes but from unwieldy and suicidal gas-filled Zeppelins. We sometimes watched them being shot down in flames and my mother cried, because she had read that some of the German crews were boys of sixteen. Somehow this seemed to have very little connexion with the science I was learning, but it may have had something to do with my own growing feeling that war was utterly wrong.

When I became a research student, training under Sir William Bragg in the very place where Sir Humphry Davy, Michael Faraday, John Tyndall, Sir James Dewar, and other world-famous scientists had carried out their research, the war was over and, as we thought, won. We genuinely hoped for a peace settlement that would end all war. Terrible things had happened, but we believed that there were plenty of good Germans, and that they would now have a chance to come out on top. Terrible things had happened and were perhaps still happening in Russia, but other countries, America and France, for instance, had had pretty ghastly revolutions too, and then settled down. It might take time. Meanwhile my work was fun. I often ran the last few yards to the laboratory. Later on I took my mathematical calculations with me to the nursing-homes where my babies were born; it was exciting to find out new facts.

Now science seems to have become something of a Frankenstein. Chunks of it have become secret; slightly indecent, as it were. For a time, indeed, during the war and for a few years after, secrecy became a disease. If a discovery had any practical value at all, it must be kept secret. If good, it must not be shared with our enemies or competitors. If bad, they must not be allowed to copy it or to discover the antidote. What does this enmity and competition involve?

Scientific discoveries of any kind are certainly a power and a responsibility. The world's resources are very unevenly distributed. If a new use is found for some raw material that is the monopoly of one or a few nations, those nations may become wealthy overnight, or they may become a prey to more powerful neighbours. That was brought home to me very forcibly after World War II. I had gone to give lectures in Paris. My husband went to a scientific congress in Brussels. The shortages of food and of almost all other commodities were still acute in France. Not so, apparently, in Belgium. Why? Both had suffered during the war. But Belgium now had uranium to sell, from rich mines in the Belgian Congo. France was obliged to export her dairy produce. The uranium from Belgium was going to the USA for dollars, and some of it was sold to Britain.

Where was the Soviet Union to get uranium? No doubt she had some, and was busy prospecting to find more. There was some in Poland, too. But there were also rich uranium mines in Czechoslovakia. It was rather important not to let that go West, if the Soviet Union were eventually to compete on equal terms in the making of nuclear weapons and the production of power from nuclear fuel. There was a strong communist minority in Czechoslovakia, too, strong enough to seize power, with Soviet backing just around the corner. In fact, the Czechoslovakian *coup d'etat* of 1948, which shocked and alarmed the West, and which has poisoned East-West international relations ever since, was an almost inevitable consequence of the dropping of the first two atomic bombs on Hiroshima and Nagasaki. It might have been expected. It could hardly have shocked intelligent politicians.

Of course it was deplorable. Although conditions have improved recently, no-one visiting Prague can pretend that this is a light-hearted, happy city. But I simply do not see how a nation such as Britain that believes in the policies of 'Peace through strength' and of 'Negotiation from strength', that holds on to unwilling colonies because they are important strategic bases or because they have important raw materials, could really have expected the Soviet Union to behave any differently. They are no better than we are. Why should they be? They believe in 'Negotiation from strength' too.

The enormous speed of scientific development during the past fifty years has meant a revolution in means of transport and communications, the mechanization of factories and homes, and the production of hideously destructive scientific weapons of war. Two developments are bound to follow. The first is that the next fifty or one hundred years are certain to bring other spectacular advances. The second is that some, at least, of the countries that are at present technically under-developed will undoubtedly catch up with the West, as the Soviet Union is now doing.

The material prosperity and military power of any nation is dependent upon its possession of raw materials and on its scientific and technical development. Those countries which as yet have few scientists, technologists, and technicians and have not built roads, railways, and power stations are technically under-developed even though they may have a long and honourable history and a high degree of culture: Whether they can become technically developed depends upon their possession of raw materials that can be traded for revenue, or upon the assistance of wealthier nations, or upon their having some means of attracting investment capital from their own or other people. There is no reason whatever why they should not, with expert help, be able to produce scientists, though of course it will take time. Japan did it. China is training scientists and technicians at a great rate, many of whom are ploughed back into teaching. Iraq is planning to spend some millions of her oil revenue on the building of roads. Egypt has failed to attract the capital she needs for the construction of the Aswan High Dam, although without technical development and irrigation, plus good government of course, it is impossible for the mass of her people to live at anything more than a sub-human level.

In general, the lack of technical development means that the majority of the country's inhabitants do live miserably poor lives. Sometimes, if the weather is good and the soil rich, as in parts of Thailand, so that clothes and shelter, apart from shade, are unimportant, and food is fairly easily come by, life may not be too unendurable, provided that one's wants are few. But in places like China, where it can be very cold, very hot, or very wet, where floods and drought alternate and the population is too large for the amount of agricultural land available, the conditions under which many people have had to live are so ghastly that they must be seen to be believed. In such a case it is absolutely essential that the power consumption per man – the general availability of electrical and mechanical power – shall be increased. Besides, the Asians are beginning to want bicycles, radios, refrigerators, and good drainage systems too.

Britain, with some 2 per cent of the world's population, is using some 10 per cent of the world's power.

India, with over 17 per cent of the world's population, is using only 1½ per cent of the world's power.

This is the main reason for the difference in the standards of living in these two countries.

In China one can still see groups of men, women, and children working a kind of treadmill in order to raise water from the streams to the level of the fields. They have to work hard for hours to irrigate an acre. No wonder that the collective farms that have been able to acquire a mechanical pump can get bigger yields for less effort. We must not forget that many of the manmade wonders of the past – the Pyramids of Egypt, the Taj Mahal of India, the Temple of Heaven of Peking, the wonders of Greek and Roman architecture – were built by men who were either slaves or no better off than slaves.

Power is not something that need necessarily continue in short supply, but fuel is not evenly distributed, and it can be used up. Britain has been fortunate in having had ample supplies of coal and iron, but her coal is running out. Less easily mined seams are now being worked. The industry has been nationalized partly because although essential it was beginning not to pay. The best coal had been creamed off. Governments must look ahead in terms of centuries, and our coal will not last more than another couple of centuries even at its present rate of consumption, which must increase if we are to compete in the world's markets and maintain our own standards of living too.

What other sources are there? The sun? It may be possible to harness the energy of the sun, and even perhaps to store it, in those countries that get enough sunshine; but Britain does not. It is certainly very desirable indeed, from the point of view of the power-hungry countries, that research, guided and financed internationally perhaps, shall investigate the practical possibilities of utilizing solar energy.

Wind? We have had windmills for many centuries, but the quantities of power that can be generated in this way are too small for modern requirements: but again, research into new methods of utilization needs stimulating and encouraging. Tides? We have those in Britain, but (according to the late Sir Francis Simon) the maximum saving to be gained by harnessing the tides would be only about 2 per cent of our coal consumption at a cost of some £200 million. We could, if we wanted to, save up to 20 per cent at a cost of under £10 million, by getting rid of our open grates and installing closed stoves. This would still not solve our power problem.

We do not, in Britain, have the mountainous catchment areas that would provide us with sufficient hydro-electric power for our needs, although if capital were available some really enormous schemes of this kind could be put into operation in some of the technically backward areas. One such, suggested by Dr Hans Thirring, by harnessing the waters of the Tsangpo River, in Eastern Tibet, could provide up to 333,000 million kilowatt-hours of electricity annually.

We in Britain are importing oil to supplement our coal, mostly hitherto from the Arab states. Coal and oil are essential not only for our power supplies but also as source materials for our chemical and metallurgical industries: and they need to be conserved for that purpose. But imported goods are precarious.

The consumption of Europe as a whole in 1975 is likely to be over 1,000 million tons of coal. In order to replace coal gradually and to supplement it as our supplies run short, we plan to use power from nuclear fuel. We are building and putting into operation nuclear power stations. This is a considered decision involving large sums of public money and there is no doubt that nuclear power has come to stay. It brings with it hideous problems, problems of which both scientists and politicians are aware. Risks can be minimized and of course are being minimized, but they exist. What are they?

Well, there are the scientific risks. Nuclear fission is the breakdown of the nuclei of certain heavy elements with the release of primary and secondary energy in the form of heat, light, and pressure waves. In addition, large quantities of special kinds of high-energy radiation are generated and these will include two or three neutrons violently ejected from each atom broken up, and the highly radioactive fragments – the fission products – of the divided nuclei. The ejected neutrons can act as projectiles causing a chain of further similar fission processes, and this chain reaction can be either controlled, as in the nuclear pile, or catastrophic, as in the atom bomb.

The risk of a nuclear pile, used for power production, accidentally getting out of control is very small indeed, smaller than the risk that a coal mine may become ignited, but both risks exist. It is a tragedy when coal miners lose their lives through an accident, but the effect of the vaporization of the material of a large nuclear reactor in a highly populated area would be much more terrible. Even if it were not a highly populated area, many people would be killed, and a large area contaminated for a long time, with devastating effects on agricultural production.

Then there is the disposal of the radioactive waste from the atomic energy industrial processes.

In a nuclear power station it is the heat that is used to generate useful electrical or mechanical energy, through the medium of a heat engine. The by-products, in the form of high-energy radiation and fission products, must be used or disposed of somehow. Some of the particles can be reabsorbed in order to breed new fissile material, some can be used to provide isotopes and radioactive substances of various kinds for research, for all sorts of useful medical and industrial purposes. But one pound of uranium gives long-lived radioactivity comparable with that from about half a ton of radium: and four ounces of radium are sufficient to treat several thousand patients every year.

As with strawberries and cream, too much of a good thing is an embarrassment. Some by-products of a nuclear power plant can be exported and used for beneficial purposes by other countries that have no nuclear piles of their own. The new fissile material could be used as fresh fuel for the power station. Unfortunately it can also be stockpiled for the making of nuclear weapons. But even then there is still an enormous quantity of dangerous waste material to be got rid of. When all the electrical power in Britain comes from heat generated by the fission of uranium, the radiation to be disposed of somehow will be as much as that from about a million tons of radium. Or, to put it in another way, there will be several million gallons of highly dangerous waste materials to be dumped somewhere even within the next twenty-five years,[2] and there are gaseous fission products which must be either reduced to liquid or solid form, or released under very carefully controlled conditions.

These problems are being faced by all the countries that are now developing or proposing to develop power from nuclear fuel. The effects of radiation on crops, on animals, on marine life and on man himself are being studied and research in these fields will and must be stepped up, because we still have to admit ignorance in many very important respects. The last four sentences in a Report to the Public on *The Biological Effects of Atomic Radiation* published in 1956 by the US National Academy of Sciences are as follows:

'Obviously, it will not do to let nuclear plants spring up *ad lib* over the earth. The development of atomic energy is a matter for careful, integrated

2 The US Report (National Academy of Sciences) on *Disposal and Dispersal of Radioactive Wastes,* gives the total as 200 million gallons by 1980 and 2,400 million gallons by the year 2000. Some concentration would be possible but very expensive.

planning. A large part of the information that is needed to make intelligent plans is not yet at hand. There is not much time left to acquire it.'

At present, radioactive waste products are being stored in tanks or pits in the ground, carried out to sea in containers and dumped, or discharged into large river systems. In England we are piping them into the Irish Sea. Probably no serious damage has yet been done to marine life. The sea is vast and deep. But as nuclear power production is stepped up, the processes of isolation and dispersion of these dangerous materials will certainly have to be made the subject of international agreement.

Every country with a coastline is surrounded by coastal waters over which there is a large measure of national jurisdiction. But the one thing no Government can prevent is the gradual interchange of surface waters and the movement of plant and animal life in the sea. This can be proved by anyone with a bath and a fountain pen. If a drop of ink is deposited at one end of the bath, even in such stagnant water it will soon be dispersed so as slightly to colour the whole.

Measurements were carried out after the test explosions of nuclear weapons in the Pacific Ocean in 1954. There is always a certain small amount of natural radioactivity in the sea, mostly due to a radioactive form of the element potassium. Two days after the tests the radioactivity of the surface waters near Bikini was a million times greater than normal. Ocean currents, about which we still know far too little, helped to spread the contaminated water and four months later waters 1,500 miles from Bikini had three times as much radioactivity as their usual value.

All this time the radioactivity itself would be dying away – decaying – much as the hotness of a bath decays while we lie in it. Some kinds of atoms lose their radioactivity very quickly indeed, others much more slowly. One of the most dangerous of the fission products, radioactive strontium, has a comparatively long life. It loses half its activity in 10,000 days. So that while the contaminated water moved away from the test area, the radiation itself would be decreasing, fast at first and then more slowly. Yet thirteen months later the water 3,500 miles away showed a small, but definite rise of radioactivity. It is not possible to say how much marine life may have suffered in the neighbourhood of the area or what degree of radioactivity is necessary before immediately or genetically harmful effects result. But what does seem certain is that the total amounts of radioactive waste that will eventually have to be disposed of, as safely as possible, when there are nuclear power stations all over the world, will be even greater than the amounts that would be let loose, deliberately and devastatingly, in a nuclear war.

CHAPTER 3

Even from the scientific point of view, therefore, it seems clear that absolute national sovereignty cannot be maintained in a world that wishes to avoid slow but certain deterioration of human health and well-being. For that is what is involved if we steadily or catastrophically expose ourselves to large quantities of high-energy radiation, over and above the natural amounts that come from the earth and from space. We increase our own liability to blood and intestinal disorders and later in life to leukemia and cancer. We increase the likelihood that children in future generations will be born with inherited defects, some really serious ones. We destroy or depreciate our food supplies if we contaminate agricultural land or fishing waters.

No nation can claim that it can do what it likes, even with its own. The air above it will move to other parts of the world. The water around it will be exchanged gradually, not only with surface waters elsewhere, but also with the waters in the depths of the ocean. 'No man is an island', indeed. To be internationally-minded is a matter of enlightened self-interest rather than of morals. It pays to come to an agreement with other nations whom you may harm and who may harm you, or with whom you might share certain benefits.

Enlightened self-interest is not morality, yet morality would have come to the same conclusion, perhaps by a quicker or less painful route. When Quaker shopkeepers, because of a concern for truth, introduced fixed prices they gained much custom. Would-be buyers found that they could send a child or any other messenger and get the same quality goods as if they went themselves. And pretty soon, of course, fixed prices became the custom among other shopkeepers because it paid. Honesty was, and is, the best policy.

So is international co-operation. The World Meteorological Organization (WMO), which is one of the Specialized Agencies of the United Nations, has a membership considerably greater than that of the United Nations itself, not only because it pays to belong to it but because it pays to have the co-operation in it of as many countries as possible. It pays not to keep others out. Weather is one of the most important factors in many large-scale projects. Meteorological services help to increase food yields by answering questions relating to planting, cultivating, harvesting, processing, and shipping and by expanding production to areas previously barren or undeveloped. Wind forecasts and storm warnings help fishing fleets to know which areas can be safely worked. Frost, floods, thunderstorms, and the movements of typhoons can be predicted. Aviation and other forms of transport are made safer by such foreknowledge.

The International Telecommunication Union and the Universal Postal Union, two other Specialized Agencies, are obviously desirable forms of international co-operation for the provision of efficient country-to-country services at the cheapest possible rates.

The World Health Organization is another Specialized Agency with a very large membership: because clearly it is to the benefit of all nations to work for 'the attainment by all peoples of the highest possible level of health', and to break the vicious circle of 'sickness-breeds-poverty-breeds-sickness'. Plagues are no respecters of sovereignty. When, in 1947, cholera broke out in Egypt and every day was bringing 1,000 new cases and 500 deaths, twenty nations co-operated to form a supply line for vaccines and other drugs. Within ten weeks the epidemic was checked.

Even now, however, most of the world's two thousand five hundred million inhabitants are suffering from some form of ill-health that might be prevented, cured, or at least alleviated. Three of the worst scourges are malaria, the venereal diseases, and tuberculosis. Many scientists think that all three might be eliminated. Some diseases, such as cancer, we do not yet know how to prevent. Where knowledge is available there is still a grievous lack of trained people to put that knowledge into practise. One way of looking at it is to realize that most of the world is now in much the same state as were the labouring classes in Great Britain a century or more ago: malnutrition, overcrowding in bad sanitary conditions, large families, high infantile mortality, chronic ill-health, periodic epidemics.

The modern public-health movement originated in England, about 1850, with an epoch-making report by Sir Edwin Chadwick entitled 'The sanitary condition of the labouring population of Great Britain'. Chadwick's successor, Sir John Simon, in his first annual report as Medical Officer of Health for the City of London, wrote:

> I feel the deepest conviction that no sanitary system can be adequate to the requirements of the time, or can cure those radical evils which infest the under-framework of society, unless the importance be distinctly recognized, and the duty manfully undertaken, of improving the social conditions of the poor.

When sub-standard conditions are removed, some diseases disappear or lose their virility. Nearly fifty years ago, the Health Officer of Glasgow found that in one-room tenements the case rate during an epidemic of measles was 125 per 1,000 and the death rate 27 per 1,000: in four-room tenements the corresponding figures were 11 and 1 per thousand. In China to-day many families are still fixing with eight or more people in one mudwalled, mud-floored room, and whether we like their present form of government or not, it is a fact that only now is this shocking state of affairs being really seriously tackled. It remains to be seen if housing reform can catch up with the enormous rate of increase of the population.

One thing is quite sure: and any would-be reformer must face it. It is not possible for the world population to expand indefinitely and not starve. Simple arithmetic is convincing.

If each two parents have four children who in turn become parents (that is, excluding those who die young, or who have no children of their own) then the world's population must double in each generation. Suppose we allow three generations to each century, then an average family of four fertile children would mean that the world's population of 2,500 million would become about 20,000 million by 2,050, about 160,000 million by 2,150, and over 1 million millions by 2,250, three centuries from now. It seems absurd, and of course it is.

Whatever limit we may set to the food-producing capacity of the earth, whatever marginal areas we bring into production, whatever use we make of food from the sea, whatever synthetic foods we may manufacture from wood or coal or anything else, the limit would have been reached long before that time. Yet three centuries is not very long. Quite a number of people can trace their family trees farther back than that. The Society of Friends has held to its Peace Testimony for over 300 years. Some of us hope to see our great-grandchildren. Three hundred years is only nine generations.

Another way of visualizing the problem is to calculate how long it would be before the world population actually covered the earth. Taking the radius of the earth as 4,000 miles, the total surface area (sea, Arctic regions and all) is about 620 million million square yards. The present population is 2,500 million. If it were to double itself in each generation, there would be one person per square yard in six centuries. Absurd, no doubt, but there it is. Of course they would mostly have died of starvation long before that stage of overcrowding.

Yet an average family of four child-bearing children was by no means a surprising thing in Britain a century, or even half a century ago. Elizabeth Fry had eleven children within fifteen years. I myself was the youngest of ten; four died in infancy and of the remaining six, two were childless, but four became parents in turn. Such large families were a commonplace, even though Malthus had long published his famous Essay on Population. No-one felt apologetic about it.

It seems pretty certain that prehistoric or early man obeyed the edict 'Be fruitful and multiply': to have a quiverful of children was to be blessed. That makes it all the more curious to realize that in fact for hundreds of centuries the rate of increase of the world population must have been very slow indeed.

This, too, can be proved by simple arithmetic. If N is the original number of human beings (not less than two! Adam and Eve, if you like) and x is the number of child-bearing children in each family, then after y generations the world population would be

$$N \times (x/2) \times (x/2) \times (x/2)\, y \text{ times.}$$

If x is 2 the population remains absolutely stationary; if x is 4 it doubles in every generation and increases at the enormous rate of (eight times) in every century. Now it is estimated that the world population three centuries ago, in A.D. 1650, was about 500 million. Let us suppose that y is at least 300: that means that man, as a tool-using animal, had lived on the earth for at least one hundred centuries before A.D. 1650. Then

$$N\,(x/2)300 = 500,000,000$$

This can easily be solved using logarithms. Taking

N = 2 we find that $x/2 = 1.07$ or $x = 2.14$.
If N = 2,000 then $x/2 = 1.03$ or $x = 2.06$.

In other words, the average number, all over the world, of children who grew up to become parents was not much more than two in each family. There was no likelihood of any birth control other than a primitive form of abortion. The fact was that life was so hard, so precarious, so cruel, that relatively few children did grow up, out of all that were born.

That is what would happen again if the population outgrew its food supplies. Health services or no health services, children would starve and die. There would undoubtedly be competition for what agricultural land there is, but starving men are no match for modern scientific weapons; and the technically developed nations, if not squeamish and if not divided, would certainly win a war fought against relatively unarmed men, however numerous.

But they might not be unarmed. Nevertheless, whoever was the victor the problem would remain. Man must not outgrow his living space, and if he has an average family of more than two healthy child-bearing children he soon will. And that is just what is happening to-day in some parts of the world.

It is sometimes hopefully assumed that men and women will become less fertile when they are better fed. Evidence has been put forward relating high fertility to lack of protein in the diet, or showing that the bigger the small holding, the smaller the family. If all other factors could be eliminated, such evidence might be convincing. The fact that the population of the USA is now increasing rather fast makes haywire of this kind of statistics, because even the poorest people in the USA are pretty well off compared with those of, say, Egypt or China. It is far more likely that where families are relatively smaller, for example in the slightly better-fed families in Japan, it is because they do deliberately control the size of their families; not because they are less fertile. It is also suggested that famine conditions favour small families and therefore the infecund would survive through a process of natural selection. This kind of stabilization of the world population, which depends upon the incidence of recurring famine, is hardly likely to eliminate competition between nations for what supplies there are.

I have laboured this point because I believe it to be an absolutely vital one. It is sometimes even argued – perhaps it is arguable on a strictly logical basis – that the growing irradiation of the human race, not only by nuclear weapons tests but by the increasing use of X-rays, radium, radiocobalt, and so on, and by the controlled release of radioactive by-products, might actually be beneficial in producing increased sterility, even at the expense of a somewhat higher proportion of tragically defective children and of disease later in life.

That is surely an unnecessarily callous solution to the problem. If children are to be born at all, the whole world should see to it, if it is possible, that they are healthy, that they have a healthy, happy childhood, that they grow up to be healthy, happy, useful adults and die without unnecessary suffering. This is not always admitted; and I am not arguing that suffering, bravely borne, may not be ennobling or creative. It often is. What I do argue is that we should not deliberately add to it, and if that is not admitted then we are arguing from different premises.

What then is to be done about countries like Japan, China, or India, where the populations are increasing at such a rate that, whatever measures of social improvement are undertaken, it seems as if these countries must sooner or later burst their bounds? Take Japan, for example. According to their census returns, Japan's population was 72,000,000 in 1945, 83,200,000 in 1950 and 89,300,000 in 1955. The increase over ten years was more than three times the total population of Switzerland. Part of the early increase was due to the repatriation of Japanese ex-servicemen and other overseas residents. The birth-rate in 1945 was actually exceeded by the death rate. But this trend was soon reversed and although the birth-rate is coming down pretty sharply, the death rate has also fallen until it is very nearly as low as in the Western countries. The natural increase rate, which is the difference between the two, is still above one per cent per annum. This does not seem much perhaps, until it is realized that one per cent per annum means 270 per cent per century, since it must be counted like compound interest.

This is not all. The decline in the birth-rate that has occurred is, according to the Japanese Ministry of Welfare, due partly to birth control, but even more to legalized abortion. Birth control, says Ayanori Okasaki, the Director of the Institute of Population Problems, became almost a mania after the war; and at the same time, and probably because of the availability of contraceptives and of information about their use, there was an alarming deterioration in sexual morality. The Eugenics Protection Law of 1948, which made legal the sale of contraceptives, also, after its revision in 1952, permitted induced abortions by responsible doctors with the agreement of both husband and wife. The result was that in 1954 there were reported 1,143,059 induced abortions to 1,765,126 actual births, and in 1955 the registered abortions reached the record figure of 1,727,040. Not at all a healthy state of affairs.

What has this to do with peace? A very great deal. Pacifists and other peace-loving people are too apt to think in terms of slick solutions of world problems, if indeed they think of them at all. What I have been trying to emphasize is that one major world problem is the growth of population, whether in technically developed, or in technically under-developed countries.

Japan is a technically developed country. It really has very little agricultural land. Most of it is mountainous and either wooded or barren. What arable land there is, is intensively cultivated. Travelling by train one sees the little strips of land being farmed right down to the railway track and in terraces as high up the mountains as is possible. The average area of cultivated land per farming household in Japan is 2 acres, as compared with 124 acres in Germany, 21 in France, 48 in USA, and 80 in Denmark. The soil is not particularly good, either. The wheat yield per acre in Japan is only one-third of that in Denmark. The rice yield is less than that from the same areas in Italy or Spain. The total area that can be cultivated is under 15 million acres, or less than one-fifth of an acre per person, yet at British yields it would take 1½ acres to feed one person properly. (Less, however, if he is a vegetarian!) The Japanese *must* import food and of course they supplement their diet with a good deal of fish. But they must export manufactured goods to pay for their imports of food and raw materials or else they must overflow somehow, somewhere, or else they must starve.

We in Britain do not like the economic competition of 'the little yellow men', as we sometimes contemptuously call them. Of course it is unfair competition. Their working conditions are much worse than ours, so that they can and do undercut us in the market for cheap quality goods.

They have attempted to overflow several times. They succeeded in overflowing to Manchuria and to North Korea. These have been taken away again. They tried, and nearly succeeded in the attempt, to conquer China and exploit her resources. They would like to emigrate to Australia. It is hardly surprising that Australia does not want them. 'It is all their own fault', said a wealthy Australian woman to me, on the aeroplane going from Bangkok to Melbourne, 'they shouldn't have so many children.'

That is the slick solution. They shouldn't have so many children. Well, they are trying not to: and since birth control is not always as effective as advertised (at least not when practised by a rural, inexperienced population) and self-control seems too much to expect from most ordinary human beings, the result is over one million seven hundred thousand legalized abortions, apart from those illegally performed and not reported. And still the population is increasing.

I don't know the answer. Do you? Is war the answer? Two of the questions that I was asked two years ago in Japan by a group of young Japanese women were: 'What sort of training can we give our children that will make them welcome as immigrants in other countries?' 'How can we teach them that war is wrong?'

These women do not want a return to militarism, in spite of the fact that to them the Korean war was a godsend (if one may use such a phrase in such a connexion). It provided employment for Japan's heavy industries, which had been stepped up for the war that they called the 'China Affair', and which were likely to be stepped down again by Japan's enforced disarmament. Japan became the arsenal of the East and her unemployment figure is now comparatively low. But most Japanese working people feel that unemployment is never very far away.

A Japanese student whom I had advised to work a little less hard and to enjoy the architectural beauties of Paris while he had the chance, replied, most devastatingly, 'But, Mrs Lonsdale, in my country it is not a virtue to enjoy oneself.' The Buddhist religion teaches that the object of human life should be to secure freedom from want by not wanting very much. All the same, most people do want economic as well as military security, and we are teaching them, by example, if not by sharing, to want the luxuries that we have, as well.

We *are* sharing. I do not want to undervalue the idealism that is basic to much of the work of the United Nations. Take the Food and Agricultural Organization, for example. It grew out of the Hot Springs Conference held in the USA in May 1943, when 44 nations agreed to work together to secure a lasting peace through freedom from want. They agreed that:

Two-thirds of the world's people are under-nourished.

Their health could be vastly improved if they were able to get enough of the right kind of food.

The farmers of the world – two-thirds of its population – could produce enough if they used the best agricultural methods.

Full-time work for all could be provided by increased production and efficient distribution.

The nations must act together to attain these ends. They have acted together to a limited extent. Countries which join the FAO pledge themselves to attempt to do away with famine and malnutrition. Their major work has been in providing expert technical advice and training. Funds have not been available for the actual buying and distribution of food, fertilizers or farming machinery, nor has FAO authority to do these things, but it has laid down principles for the disposal of food surpluses and the Economic and Social Council is planning what can be done to meet food shortages as they arise.

The United Nations Children's Fund, well known as UNICEF, is doing much more than giving material relief. It is giving hope, encouraging self-help, and initiating projects of lasting value, such as national and child welfare training services, milk conservation plants, anti-tuberculosis campaigns, as well as giving emergency help to child victims of famine or flood.

I have taken these only as examples.

Yet because these forms of mutual help are so valuable it is all the more pity that we in Britain support them so inadequately. The United Nations, according to the head of the Technical Assistance Board, spends three times as much in Britain, buying know-how, as Britain contributes to the United Nations for technical assistance projects. To be sure, there is also the Colombo Plan. But examination of the official account of National Income and Expenditure, prepared by the Central Statistical Office, and published by Her Majesty's Stationery Office, shows that in 1955 the net current grants from overseas governments to Britain were £44 million, while current grants paid to overseas governments and to international organizations were only £59 million.

In the same year we spent £1,576 million on military defence, excluding civil defence, war pensions and service grants, war damage compensation, post-war credits, and national debt interest. £1,576 million for defence, less than £59 million for international co-operation! One would have thought that even as payment on an insurance policy the amount was somewhat contemptible.

We have refused our immediate support for the proposed Special UN Fund for Economic Development (SUNFED), to be used for the financing of public works projects essential for promoting industrial and agricultural expansion, such as building roads, housing, schools, and hospitals in needy countries. We claim that it must wait for international agreement on disarmament! The USSR disagrees, and it is possible that the Fund will be established without our support, but with that of the Soviet Union. One would have supposed that enlightened self-interest alone would have reasoned that this is pure folly on our part.

CHAPTER 4

I can't leave this question of population, because one of the objects of military alliances and military defence seems to be the prevention of population movements, the freezing of the *status quo*.

It is just not possible to freeze the *status quo*, either nationally or internationally. One might as well try to freeze the Indian Ocean. The present inequalities of living standards are too great to be frozen in and the present inequalities of population densities will soon be greatly accentuated.

A war cannot maintain unsatisfactory situations; it changes them, but it is not the best or only way of changing them. It can, of course, remove a dictator or a government. It cannot solve problems that are the results of inevitable world trends. I doubt very much whether even a war fought with hydrogen bombs, if we were wicked enough to use them, would stop the growth of the Chinese people. A dozen hydrogen bombs coated with uranium 238, like that tested on 1 March 1954, could blanket Great Britain with a lethal fall-out; but Great Britain is small enough to be swallowed up many times over in China. If we killed off one hundred million Chinese people in and around their major cities, there would still be over five hundred million left: and life for most of them could hardly be any grimmer than it has been in the past. The fall-out would come back to us in our turn, and our descendants, as well as theirs, would pay for our folly.

There are signs that the Chinese government is beginning to be aware of the problems that a rapidly growing population will pose for themselves and for their successors.[3] I am sure that they will soon be well aware of it. With

3 See *Observer* 9 September 1956.

the growth of health services, the provision of better living conditions, the improvement of nutrition, and the training of adequate numbers of doctors and nurses, this growth of population will be accentuated by a drop in the death rate, unlikely to be compensated for in several decades, at least, by any correspondingly dramatic fall in the birth-rate. We cannot solve this problem for them. We certainly do not help them to solve this or any other problem having grave international repercussions by refusing to allow the present Chinese Government to take its seat in the councils of the United Nations. One would have supposed that a responsible international outlook was something to be encouraged. Whatever privileges may accrue to active membership of the UN, whatever awkwardness might result from having another, and powerful, communist voice there, are as nothing compared with the desirability that the People's Republic of China shall co-operate with, and not be withdrawn or banished from, the family of nations as a whole.

It may very well be that this problem of population is one that the communist nations will have to face mutually. When I was in China, I certainly met many Chinese people who, on being told that all their efforts at social improvement were like those of a man trying to catch up with a train gathering speed, were convinced that they would be able to spill over into Mongolia and Siberia, and that these areas would welcome them. That will be as it may be. They were equally convinced that they would not attempt to solve their population problem by force. 'We have had force used against us many times,' said a leading Chinese Christian to me, 'and although apparently successful for a time, it has always failed in the long run. Is it likely that we would adopt a method that we know is foredoomed to failure? We would defend ourselves, but we would never be aggressors.'

Well, that again depends on the definitions of defence and of aggression. Is gradual infiltration aggression?

The question that faces a practical pacifist is just how to replace wars of aggression and of defence as a means of readjusting populations that can no longer be confined within their original bounds. It is too late to question the wisdom of spreading knowledge of health measures. It is spread. The wisdom of doing so *has* been questioned only, I think, in order to draw attention to the continuing problem. Such knowledge cannot for long be hidden, in any case.

The greatest danger to peace is not from a nation like India which, although increasing in numbers rapidly, is neither technically strong enough, nor constitutionally belligerent enough to attempt to increase her territory or to force other nations to receive her nationals. It is very true that India and Pakistan may quarrel over Kashmir, or India and Portugal over Goa. It is unlikely that either of these disputes will flare up into war, and highly improbable that if they did, the war would spread. It is also true that Indian immigrants can cause trouble between India and other countries to which they migrate, such as South Africa. All kinds of conflicts and disputes are bound to arise. The more representative and less partisan the United Nations, the more successful the work of its specialized agencies, the more likely it is that such disputes will be referred there or to the World Court of Justice, and the less likely that their decisions or advice will be flouted; although here it is essential that the Great Powers set a good example, which is just what Britain has not always done.

A far greater danger is from the technically developed nations. The Japanese people may be able, by the very drastic methods they have evolved for themselves, to stabilize their population, certainly at a considerably higher level than at present, but almost equally certainly at lower standards of living. If we are crazy enough, as we are at present, to encourage them to violate or bypass their constitution and rearm themselves, they can hardly be expected not to become a menace again in the East. No-one who has seen what they did in China or who has met any of the British prisoners who were in the power of the Japanese can doubt their capacity for cruelty and ruthlessness. Let not our remorse, if we feel any, at the dropping of the first atom bombs make us think that Japanese militarists or their human tools are misunderstood angels. The Japanese women do not think so. They dread the reimposition or reintroduction of militarism in their country.

If, in spite of us, they do avoid warlike attempts to attain living space, what other avenues are there? Again, it seems to me, the answer depends to a large extent on the stature and universality of the United Nations; on the degree to which it is supported, not by military power, but by the respect and willing co-operation of its members. A nation that wanted to avoid wars of expansion, but was at its wit's end to know how to balance its budget and to feed itself, might very well, and without any humiliation, ask for the advice or criticism of the rest of a *friendly* world. In a world in which war had become unthinkable, that would be a perfectly natural thing to do. Without push-ing the analogy too far, we may remember that that is what Malta has done in asking for help from the British Government. Such situations will, I am sure, become increasingly frequent as countries become too civilized to use the methods of modern mass-slaughter.

If, however, the boot were on the other foot, and advice was not sought but was obviously needed, it could be given only if the relationships between the nations were sound and wholesome, as they are in a well-regulated family. Even in the best regulated families, however, parents do sometimes disagree, and children, particularly in the growing and adolescent stage, feel themselves to be thwarted and refuse to take well-meant advice or to submit to disci-pline. Refusal to use force in such a case is not a sign of parental weakness. It is a sign of family strength for the members to be able to live with their disagreements and to outlive them.

A great deal depends upon the example set by those who regard themselves as being the more experienced and mature. If those who are the strongest, having used their strength and ability to attain a position of authority, con-tinue to use them to protect what they regard as their own interests, they must expect that younger or weaker members of the family of nations will learn, as they grow stronger, to use the same methods, and if they are bigger, will probably use them even more effectively.

Is this what we really want? Never mind what we think *will* happen. Do we really want the technically under-developed nations, as they grow stronger, to concentrate on their own interests, as we in the West have done?

It is natural enough. Without the benefit of good example, and training in better, more co-operative ways, children are apt to be isolationist and to grab what they want for themselves. What most of the people of Asia are now demanding is not only independence from colonizing powers, but also independence from exploitation within their own communities, many of which are still of a feudalistic character. In this they have been encouraged and often used by the communists among their own numbers, who are easily able to persuade some of them that communism will give them what they want. Meanwhile their ruling classes, although far from democratic in their own sympathies, have been able to persuade the Western powers to help them, because to help *them* is to help to prevent the spread of communism. It is a fantastic situation when one really thinks about it.

The average Asian does not care about communism or about democracy. He wants to be free from the danger of starvation. He believes that colonialism and feudalism are the causes of his misery. He is confirmed in his belief by the fact that the Western powers – the colonial powers – side with his feudalistic rulers. His nationalism is a form of growing self-respect.

The average Britisher who thinks about it at all does not approve of feudalism. He wishes he could get rid of the responsibilities of colonialism but doesn't see how it could be done, since many of Britain's vital raw materials come from the colonies and other colonies are strategic points on the routes via which these raw materials are brought to him. But he feels that the Asian peasant ought to prefer Western freedom to the slavery of communism, and has to be rescued from the communists. So he sides with the feudalistic rulers to 'rescue' him. And in a sense he is at least partially right. When anti-colonialism takes the form of terrorism, the peace-loving peasant may well find himself in a cleft stick.

I have been more than interested to see the widely divergent views of the situation taken by two different Friends, both living in the East, both in most responsible University positions, both deeply concerned for justice and for right action. The one is a Japanese woman, who writes:

> The fact has been too clearly vindicated to be ignored that communism cannot be combated with arms, especially in Asia, where

anti-communism too often has its champions in the old feudalistic element of society, whose interests are tied more closely with foreign powers
than with their own people. Standing against them, nationalistic and
really democratic elements of the population are often driven into alli-
ance with communists, though they may not feel too comfortable in it.

The Cold War is essentially a conflict between the two antagonistic
economic systems. In this conflict, capitalism stands in a decidedly
handicapped position in Asia. To start with . . . the national income
is very small in Asian countries . . . This extreme poverty means that
Asia cannot afford to give ample scope for free economy . . . no-one
can deny the necessity for rationing when a limited quantity of food
has to be distributed justly.

. . . As for the terror of forced labour, even in Japan, where the national
income stands far above the average of Asian countries, there are many
housewives who devote all of their spare time (their waking hours
minus the minimum time required for housekeeping) to piecework
and can only get less than one shilling a day. Such labour is nominally
'free' and they can quit it if they like. At the same time, the work is
taken away if they complain of low payment and even this small sum is
indispensable to help support the family. When compared with such a
kind of 'free' labour, 'forced labour' may be preferable if the work and
subsistence are secured.

She goes on to discuss anti-colonialism and adds:

It is ironical that in this strife, nationalistic movements of the people
with a really democratic outlook are encouraged by the communists,
while so-called democracies ally themselves with the privileged classes
of the native population who are usually undemocratic and even reactionary in their outlook.

Indeed, many of the Westerners seem to forget that what they are trying to defend or preserve in Asia is not *their* way of life: capitalism with civil rights, social security system, etc., but a condition comparable with that of an early period after the Industrial Revolution, with its sweated labour and savage repression of the workers' efforts to combine to protect their rights.

... Here we have to admit that but for Western colonization economic development of Asia would have been much delayed, and that the native population has benefited from modern facilities of transportation, medical care, and education. Yet, it is nevertheless true that the capital invested in these regions produced far greater profit than it could ever have done in its home country, owing to the extraordinarily low wages paid to native workers.

In Malaya, which is yet to attain political independence, the annual national income shows such an incredibly high figure as $250 *per capita*. But this does not mean that all Malayans enjoy a high income. Not only is the wealth very unevenly distributed, but about $10 per head of the population is being sent out of the country as the interest on foreign investments. This situation is not exclusively applicable to colonies. Indonesia is politically independent now. Last year her government came to an agreement with the two major oil companies of the United States that they should reinvest a certain part of their profit ($60 million for Caltex and $70–80 million for Stanvac) in native industry before they were allowed to send any part of the profit out of Indonesia. This indicates two things: first, that until last year, such a vast amount of wealth gained from native resources had been flowing unlimited out of the country; and secondly, that political independence of Indonesia made it possible for her to retain at least a part of the profit for her economic development.

She goes on to point out that this is likely to mean that foreign private enterprise will be less willing to invest capital in Asia, in spite of Asia's acute need, if higher wages are to be paid to the workers and if there are to be restrictions on what the investors shall do with their profits. This, in a sense, puts Asia on the spot. Is it better to be politically independent and minus capital, or politically dependent and to be exploited? Or will the United Nations be prepared to advance capital?

If the capital necessary for economic development of Asia can be obtained through the United Nations without any political strings, she suggests:

> This will contribute both to the economic and political progress of Asia. A truly independent Asia will be a great asset to world peace. When we think of the vast sum now being squandered in arms in the futile attempt to check the spread of communism, the money to be spent in this way will be very cheap indeed compared with the effect it will bring.

My other Friend is an Englishman long resident in Singapore, who writes of conditions in Malaya:

> The Emergency here, in its early days, was a part of the general problem of controlling extortion by threat of violence. There was a good deal of extortion by threats, from gangs under varying degrees of communist or other political control, or none. The situation still retains this character, although it has become less political. I think the best-informed people believe that the attitude of the Chinese in general to the communists varies from that of fear of a protection gang at one extreme to that of payment of taxes to a secondary but not very popular government at the other: those whose support went further than this would presumably be communists, who probably do not exceed one per cent of the Chinese population. (He is referring here, of course, to the Chinese in Malaya.)

He goes on:

> At what stage does protection of individuals by the Government
> against such threats pass from a normal Government function to civil
> war? When people are frightened of giving evidence the problem is
> not easy. I am reasonably certain that it is unhelpful to deal with such
> situations by courts of law, in which only comparatively innocent
> people are likely to have witnesses against them. But if the police
> have power to detain prisoners one's attitude to co-operation with
> the police becomes a real problem. To refuse any co-operation is, in
> effect, to shelter extortion by refusing to give evidence; and puts one
> in the position of those who allow gang murders to take place in open
> streets without helping in identification. One's right to do this is surely
> limited, even where one cannot go all the way with police methods. Yet
> at some point probably one should say no ... Conditions like those in
> England, where in general it is possible to co-operate with the police
> force in giving information etc., without being involved in civil strife,
> are unhappily becoming less common; and I feel this issue poses much
> greater difficulties for a pacifist stand than ... hypothetical questions
> about invaders ravishing one's maiden aunt.

One Friend is concerned about the broad principles underlying the relationships between Asia and the West, and especially the achievement of a reasonable living standard for the lowest strata of Asian society. The other is concerned
about personal co-operation with the forces of law and order, especially where
our Western ideas of police methods cannot deal with the situation.

It is always easier to say what the United Nations should do, and what the
British nation should do in co-operation with other nations, than to decide
at what stage personal co-operation with the Government effectively means
participation in civil war; or to decide on personal behaviour of any kind.

So let me, for the time being, continue with the easier task.

CHAPTER 5

Britain was able to increase her population three- to four-fold in the nineteenth century and still to improve her standards of living, because she had clever scientists and engineers, and ample supplies of coal and steel, together with raw materials and cheap labour in her colonies. Two world wars, however, have made a vast difference to the position of Britain as a Great Power. They have meant that resources have been used up at an accelerated rate, that Britain has had to import coal and other goods for which she could not afford to pay with increased exports, and that she has become heavily dependent upon American goodwill. At the same time some parts of the British Empire have become completely independent; others are a liability because of a hostile and troublesome minority; others, while still friendly members of the British Commonwealth, are no longer a source of revenue; and it is pretty certain that sooner or later all the colonies will achieve self-government.

In spite of the fact that a long history of conscription and of military preparedness did not prevent Germany from being twice defeated, Britain decided to maintain peace-time conscription after the Second World War and to continue to spend vast sums on military preparations. Out of a combined total expenditure of £5,436 million by the Central government and by local authorities in 1955, no less than £1,576 million was spent on military defence and £30 million on civil defence.[4] As compared with these figures the police force cost £89 million, the fire service £22 million, and science and technology at university level, including all fundamental research, only about £20 million.

4 *National Income and Expenditure 1956* (HMSO). The comparable expenditures on civil defense in 1951, 2, 3, and 4 were £136M, £78M, £78M, £78 M respectively.

Our annual output of scientists is at present about 5,200, of graduate technologists about 2,800, and of technicians (Higher National Certificate and Diploma students) about 9,000. That of the Soviet Union, with four times our population, is about ten times our number of scientists (just as well-trained as ours, make no mistake about that!), eighteen times our number of graduate engineers, and about nine times our number of technicians. Good luck to them! Their country needs development, their standards of living have not yet caught up with those of Western Europe, and if they can get free from the dead-weight of war preparations there is no reason why they should not catch up; but they are not free yet. Far from it!

The position of Britain in the modern world is declining as her national resources are being used up and as her technical lead is being overtaken. She is not decrepit yet, by any means. But she has lost her first youth. Maybe one might call her middle-aged; the age, in fact, at which we expect to sober down and set a good example. When a man has lost his first youthful vigour and a woman the best of her looks, unless they are intelligent or upright or both, they begin to lose not only the admiration but even the respect of their contemporaries.

Arguing still only on the basis of enlightened self-interest, it seems incredibly foolish for a country such as ours, which is falling back into the position of a second-rate Power, to behave so unintelligently as to set a bad example to the countries which are now beginning to gain strength and independence.

It is both unintelligent and a bad example for us to spend so little on international co-operation and so much on militarism. Is that what we want the countries now becoming technically developed to do? We have promoted regional pacts that are quite out of line with the spirit of the UN Charter. Do we want similar pacts, also represented as defensive, lined up against us? We have insisted on the rearmament of Germany, against the will of a large, but now decreasing proportion of her people. According to the *US News & World Report* of 11 June 1954, opinion polls taken privately in Germany showed that whereas in 1953 only 48 per cent in the 16–25 age group were ready to serve unconditionally in a war, by 1954 the number had gone up to 63 per cent. But in the country as a whole, 49 per cent still opposed war service of any kind. The opposition to conscription among the German people themselves seems to be even greater. According to a statement made on 27 August 1956 by the Emnid Institute (the German equivalent of the Gallup Poll), some 65 per cent of all men under 65 years of age are against it, and 74 per cent of the women. A German Friend writes: 'Re-militarization is most unpopular in wide circles, and the policy of pushing it, recommended by the Western powers, is a very serious crime against the rehabilitation of Germany.'

Every time a crisis occurs in international relationships, we British seem to meet it with a military reaction, negotiation taking second place in our thoughts. Is this what we want other nations to do when they have become stronger than ourselves?

As a crowning folly, we have supposed that it is essential, for the sake of our prestige, that we should develop and explode a hydrogen bomb, just to show that we can. Are we looking forward to the day when all the newly independent, soon-to-be-technically-developed nations insist on developing their own hydrogen bombs, so that they have a big stick too? Is that what we want? Will the world be safer or more reasonable when we get it?

As a scientist I am quite frankly terrified of the widespread development of nuclear weapons. It is not a popular subject. Most people are sick of hearing about it. They are content to take the word of politicians who say that the hydrogen bomb has prevented war, even although these same politicians order mobilization to deal with, say, the Suez Canal crisis in the next breath. Negotiation from strength is a dangerously immoral position. We do not in ordinary life respect a man for his strength and bluster. In fact many big men have little wives who keep them in order. There is such a thing as moral strength and moral leadership which does not depend upon the possession of hideously destructive weapons.

I can sympathize with the average man's horror at hearing about blast, fire, and radiation. Yet I believe that in order to be capable of proper judgement and not to be swept away by emotional and easy solutions, any responsible citizen must know his facts and must have them correct.

I have said a good deal in a previous chapter about the problem of disposal of radioactive waste materials. What happens in the case of nuclear weapons?

The atomic bomb is a weapon based on the nuclear fission of heavy atoms. The damage done by energy released in the form of light, heat, and blast depends upon the circumstances of the explosion. It may be above the ground, or at ground level, or under the water. In the case of the last two, there is a widespread distribution of radioactive particles of soil and water, contaminated by the fission products, some of which are comparatively harmless, others very dangerous indeed.

Tests of these weapons may be carried out under any of these conditions, sometimes on the top of a high tower, or even high up in the atmosphere, but away from most human habitation. Animals and other living creatures are deliberately exposed to their effects in order to obtain scientific information about pathological or genetic consequences. Birds, fishes, and any other living thing in the neighbourhood will be killed, maimed, or contaminated.

The principal risk to man in the case of test explosions is from *fall-out,* the gradual deposition all over the world of the fission products. The bomb projects these high up into the air, and they may be carried great distances by the winds of the upper atmosphere; but gradually they settle out over the whole earth. The fall may begin some hours or days after the explosion, and it will continue for years. All the time the radioactivity is dying away, slowly for some kinds of atoms, fast for others. Obviously we do not need to worry much about the atoms having short-lived radioactivity, which will have died away before any fall-out of fission products begins. These fission products consist of many different kinds of atoms, but one of the most dangerous is strontium of atomic weight 90.

The reason why strontium 90 is dangerous is that it is chemically very similar to calcium. It is therefore taken up and concentrated by bone tissue, which has an affinity for calcium. It is taken up particularly easily by young bone, that is, by children. It is one of the more abundant fission products and it is a strong radiator. Yet it has a long life, reckoned in terms of a human life. Even after 28 years its radioactivity has only dropped to one-half of its original value, after 56 years to one-quarter. All this time, if absorbed into the bone, it goes on radiating internally, and it is known to cause bone tumours in experimental animals. Its action is, of course, delayed.

According to the British and American official reports, some children in both countries have already accumulated a measurable amount of radioactive strontium in their bodies. Presumably most of this has come from the milk of cows which have grazed on contaminated grassland. It is fortunate that where calcium and strontium are both present, the bone seems to prefer calcium. But in calcium-deficient conditions, strontium is of course taken up.

The quantity of strontium found in children's bones so far is quite small, only one-thousandth of what is regarded as 'safe', that is, unlikely to have any harmful effects. It would be difficult to oppose nuclear weapons tests on these grounds alone, although obviously the situation wants watching. The fall-out will continue for years even from the tests that have already taken place. So far only the USA, the USSR and Britain have carried out such tests. If they do not restrain themselves now, they will be in a very weak position to advocate restraint if and when other nations decide to develop similar weapons. And why should they not?

Once other nations have nuclear power stations, as they will have, they will also be able to make atomic bombs. The preliminary industrial processes, the mining, the purification, the preparation of the nuclear fuel are essentially the same, whether the final process is the production of industrial power or the production of weapons.

It is true that only big installations, such as Calder Hall, could be used for these dual purposes. It is true that capital, technical knowledge, and raw materials would be required. I think that we cannot suppose that we shall keep a monopoly of these things. We know, in fact, that we will not.

The American and Foreign Power Company, which is already operating eleven conventional power stations in Latin America, has opened bids for three 10-megawatt (the megawatt (MW) = 1,000,000 watts) atomic generating plants to be established there, to cost £1.4 to £1.8 million each, according to the *Financial Times*[5] which ought to know.

The Argentine, and Brazil, as well as the USA, have numerous and rich deposits of uranium.

The West German Atomic Energy Commission was formally constituted last January and hopes to build its first nuclear power plant by 1960 or 1961, to produce electricity at competitive prices; and to buy three or four reactors for research. West Germany has only a little uranium, but East Germany has some rich deposits, extensions from those in Czechoslovakia. An atomic pile is now under construction in Dresden; with Soviet help and advice an experimental reactor is also to be built in Yugoslavia; and in China reactors and fissionable material are also being supplied by the Soviet Union.

Portugal has uranium and is being assisted with her atomic development by Great Britain. So are the members of the Baghdad Pact, for whom we agreed to set up an atomic energy training centre in Baghdad. The USSR has offered to supply Egypt with nuclear materials and equipment and training facilities.

India has considerable reserves of uranium and very large amounts of readily extractable thorium. She has an atomic reactor at Bombay.

The USSR plans to build two nuclear power stations in the Ural Mountains, with a joint capacity of 1,000 MW, and another near Moscow to generate 400 MW of electricity.

The USA is presenting 20,000 kilograms of fissionable uranium to 'friendly countries' (excluding Britain) for experimental purposes, and is, of course, building up her own nuclear power station network.

And so we go on. All this could, no doubt, be quite right and proper, except for the way in which the Great Powers are using their atomic knowledge 'to win friends and influence people'. It is a dangerous game to play.

It would be quite easy to stop the tests now. Far easier than to control the making of stockpiles of nuclear weapons. The number of tests reported as

5   15 February 1956.

having taken place up to the beginning of 1956 was 67, indicating that bombs stockpiled must be of the order of some tens of thousands. According to Admiral Elis Biörkland[6] the present world production of uranium ore, of 0.28 per cent uranium content, is about 34 million tons per annum. The amounts available, at any rate as low grade ores, are almost unlimited.

Uranium ores can be detected by means of the radiation they emit. They are detected by an instrument known as the Geiger counter. They can be detected because the actual quantity of uranium in a workable deposit is very large. But this does not mean that a single bomb, or even a stockpile, could be detected at a distance, for example by an aerial survey. Stockpiles when well shielded do not give out any significant amount of radiation. An aerial survey could only detect obvious installations, large factories or perhaps mines, or of course military concentrations, airstrips, roads, railways, and harbours.

If the positions of all nuclear reactors were known, it would not be necessary to have an international authority in control to prevent the diversion of fissile material from the fuelling of the power plant to the making of nuclear weapons. A widespread mixing of scientific and technological staff of all nationalities between the various nuclear power plants in different countries might serve the same purpose far more naturally. Scientists from different countries mix very easily in a laboratory: I have had men and women of sixteen nationalities in my own. They would not feel so much like inspectors or spies (a situation that would certainly be distasteful to any scientist) if they were being actually employed by the country in which they were working, as a guarantee of good faith.

Another possibility that has been suggested is that, in order to prevent trigger-happy rulers of small states from making (and using) nuclear weapons, any fissile material that they are given or allowed to import should be 'de-natured', that is, treated, for example by dilution, so that it can be used in a power plant but not as an explosive. The power plant itself, however, gradually manufactures plutonium. This would not be de-natured and could

6 *International Atomic Policy*, George Allen and Unwin, London, 1956.

be used for making nuclear weapons. This is what we ourselves are doing with our plutonium by-product. Moreover, some small states have plenty of uranium of their own.

An internationally agreed ban of all weapon tests, however, would greatly impede the development of nuclear weapons by countries other than those that now have them. It would be self-policing, because tests cannot be concealed from the rest of the world, wherever they take place. They can be detected and located at a distance, just as earthquakes can.

The reason why we in Britain do not firmly support such a ban, but only hint that it might be possible as part of a wider scheme of disarmament, is that we are set on testing our own British hydrogen bombs and expect to do so quite soon. Indeed, when the unhappy inhabitants of the Marshall Islands petitioned the United Nations Trusteeship Council asking for a ban on nuclear tests, only the Soviet Union, India, Burma, and Syria voted in favour of such a ban; the United Kingdom and eight other Council members voted against it, holding that 'further nuclear tests were necessary for international peace and security'!

Will *you* feel secure when the nations all have nuclear weapons?

CHAPTER 6

The bomb that Britain proposes to make and test will be, or so it is reported, a fission-fusion-fission bomb; what is sometimes called a 'rigged' bomb: the most dangerous of all kinds yet produced.

This has an atomic bomb as detonator, or trigger, and a shell outside of ordinary uranium of atomic weight 238. The main body of explosive material is hydrogen: not ordinary hydrogen but, in one type of bomb anyhow, a mixture of heavy isotopes of hydrogen under high pressure, generated by a solid compound, lithium-6-deuteride.

The process in this explosive mixture is not fission but fusion, the synthesis of fight atoms to form a heavier one: the process that is believed to be the source of the heat, light, and other radiation from the sun. This fusion process can only take place at a very high temperature and hence the use of the fission (atomic) bomb to trigger it off. At the same time it produces such high-energy neutrons that they can cause the complete fission of the uranium 238 outer shell of the bomb.

The atomic bomb itself cannot exceed a maximum size, but the hydrogen bomb, whether rigged or not, can be made as big as there are means to deliver it. Since the United States Air Force[7] has confirmed that they have already successfully flown an atomic reactor in a B-36 bomber (not as a means of propulsion but for experimental purposes), this means that the maximum size of such a bomb could be very big indeed. A 20-megaton fission-fusion-fission bomb, equal in explosive power to 20 million-ton blockbusters, has already been tested. Its performance apparently exceeded

7 *The Times*, 10 January 1956.

the expectations of the scientists who designed it. It is not the biggest possible.

The fusion process produces an enormous amount of energy in the form of heat, light, blast, and direct radiation. A 20-megaton bomb would kill by heat and blast alone pretty well every living creature within a five- to ten-mile radius of its explosive centre.

But the fusion process does not give the radio-active fission products that constitute 'fall-out'. Nevertheless the combined fission-fusion-fission bomb would give a terrific amount of fallout because of the uranium that is mixed with it, or which forms its outer shell. The rigged bomb tested on 1 March 1954 sprayed a dangerous amount of fall-out over an area of over 7,000 square miles. Anyone within that area, who did not promptly remove himself into shelter and stay there, would probably die, not at once, but within a few years. The area irradiated from such a bomb is cigar-shaped downwind. Which direction that will be depends upon the wind at the time, part of which is made by the bomb. If it changes, the fission products will fall lethally elsewhere. Eight hours after the rigged bomb test, fall-out began 160 miles away, and the amount that fell in the first 36 hours was 500 rontgens, more than a lethal dose if received all at once; and it went on falling. Nearer to the bomb it would have begun sooner and the fall-out would have been heavier.

The Japanese fishermen who were inadvertently caught in the rigged bomb fall-out, one of whom died later, would *all have* died if they had not been surrounded by the ocean. This swallowed up most of the radioactive dust, so that they were only exposed to what fell on themselves and their boat. If they had promptly removed their clothes and washed off the dust, they might have avoided burns but not radiation sickness.

We should be clear, however, that the figure of 7,000 square miles is not a limited one. Farther away there would be fall-out which would begin later and would probably be entirely sub-lethal. All the same, it would cause sickness and perhaps sterility; or it would produce genetic effects in succeeding generations and increased proneness to leukemia, cancer, and anaemia in later life of those who were living at the time of the explosion.

Early in 1956, the Minister of Defence announced new plans for the dispersal of twelve million persons in Great Britain from those population centres in this country likely to be affected in the event of a global war. It was pointed out in the correspondence columns of the *Daily Telegraph* a week later that if the evacuation took place from twelve equal centres and one thousand people were moved from each every ten minutes, it would take a week to accomplish the dispersal.

Scientists, especially in the USA, have long pressed for a serious consideration of the effects of a global war; but they have not been able to agree on the wisdom or practicability of dispersal. It can certainly be strongly argued that to remove people from towns to country in Great Britain in anticipation of hydrogen bombs is likely to be a game of 'Here we go round the mulberry bush'.

Pacifists are sometimes accused of not being realistic enough. Well, let's be realistic and ask some quite important questions. If a hydrogen bomb drops on London and you have bits of seven million radioactive corpses lying around or blown all over the surrounding countryside downwind, together with strontium 90 that is going to soak into your and your baby's bones and the fall-out just goes on falling, less intensely every day to be sure, but quite inexorably, where do you go from there? To Land's End? To the Shetland Isles? Where do the rest of the fifty million inhabitants of Britain go? Will the next bomb be on Glasgow? Or Liverpool? Or perhaps on those pretty country villages near which the British nuclear weapons are stored or from which they are to be sent out? Or can they all live in deep shelters?

I am not being funny or sarcastic. Dr H. J. Muller, the Nobel Prize winner and authority on genetics, has pointed out[8] that people remaining all the time in basements of suburban houses, well-sealed off from the dust of the air outside, 110 miles downwind from an explosion of the 1 March 1954 type, would receive 100 rontgens of radiation from outside in the first week alone. If they were not in a well-sealed basement they could receive more

8 *Saturday Review*, 9 June 1956.

than ten times that amount. And he goes on to say that even doses of 50 to 100 rontgens received by an unborn baby, could give rise to permanent abnormalities of the brain, resulting in defective intelligence, such as were found, he said, in some of the children born in Hiroshima several months after the bomb had fallen. While a young person of thirty who managed to survive a dose of 1,000 rontgens, gradually accumulated, would probably die within ten years.

If we contemplate global war at all we contemplate wholesale murder and suicide. And any Civil Defence organization that ignores that fact is self-deception by a nation that seems not to want to face facts.

Civil Defence, on which we have recently been spending about four times as much as on the training of scientists and engineers, has been at least three times out of date since 1938. In that year there was a widespread expectation that gas would be used in the war that was anticipated. Gas was not used; not because everyone was issued with gasmasks, not because of prior agreements, not because of the possibility of retaliation, but because it was essentially a poor weapon. Neither side could have won the war with gas. There was a long period of 'phoney war' and the evacuees trickled back. Then there was obliteration bombing and panic.

I happened to live on the west side of London, which was comparatively quiet. Many refugees came from the east side, demanding shelter, billets for whole families, food. The Civil Defence authorities were quite unprepared for this. Our Friends' Meeting house, having kept free of the Civil Defence organization, opened its doors, provided blankets, cots, wardens, and communal meals; and we were able to help those who came to find homes. Presently the Civil Defence organization caught up and took over. By 1945 they had established very efficient firefighting procedures, hospitals standing by in case of typhus, nurses and doctors ready and so on. So had the Japanese.

But at Hiroshima the first atomic bomb overwhelmed all the Civil Defence preparations in a split second, killed or disabled a large proportion of the doctors, nurses, and fire-fighters, destroyed hospitals and fire-stations, and introduced a new terror – radioactivity.

No sooner was this state of affairs appreciated and measures introduced to cope, at least in part, with the dangers of atomic bombs, than the problem was enormously magnified by the invention of the hydrogen bomb: just the plain hydrogen bomb – unrigged. This alone would mean an area of devastation of 200 or more square miles, a plague-spot of which the best that could be hoped would be that fire would burn up the corpses that no army could bury. Even so, there might be a fringe of people who could be helped. Then the rigged bomb, the bomb that we are proposing to be able to make, introduced a new dimension again.

The flash from such a bomb would be seen instantaneously more than fifty miles away, and would give time for a quick move to shelter before the blast wave arrived. After that, the fall-out would begin and it would make an area of several thousand miles effectively uninhabitable for months. Oh yes: people could move in or out of it. But if they stayed there they would die.

> 'If seven maids with seven mops
> Swept it for half a year
> Do you suppose', the Walrus said,
> 'That they could get it clear?'
> 'I doubt it,' said the Carpenter,
> And shed a bitter tear.

If a dozen such bombs were strategically dropped on the British Isles, there would be no place to go. The pasture would be radioactive, the vegetation would be radioactive, the cow's milk would be radioactive, the buildings would be radioactive.

To spend millions on Civil Defence in the face of such facts is so fantastically stupid that one wonders who is making a good thing out of it? That, and that alone would make sense.

The fact is that nuclear war would destroy civilization as we know it, would kill perhaps a hundred million people, would cripple and deform our descendants and would settle nothing of the problems that began the war.

'Yes, yes,' I can imagine you saying, 'but calm down. We know that. That is just why we have to have these weapons. Because if we can retaliate on each other, no-one will use them. No-one would dare to.'

Is that why we spend £30 million on Civil Defence? Are we preparing for the war that isn't going to happen?

'No, no,' I can imagine you saying, 'we can't hope that there will be no more war. But at least if we all have rigged bombs, no one will use *those*. And we must be prepared for the kind of wars that will happen, so Civil Defence is still indispensable.'

CHAPTER 7

The exercise I have tried to set myself in the first place is to think in practical terms, realistically. It seems to me, then, that only the following kinds of war are possible:

1. Global war fought with every weapon available.
2. Global war fought with limited weapons.
3. Minor wars fought with small atomic weapons.
4. Minor wars fought without atomic weapons.

It is agreed that global war of type 1 would be both murder and suicide and is unthinkable. For the time being, however, that is what the Great Powers are preparing for, both in respect of rigged bomb tests and in respect of military expenditure, a considerable amount of which is on the development of major weapons. They have not yet been able to agree on any degree of limitation.

A great deal of thought, both diplomatic and scientific, has been expended on the problem of international control and inspection, so that if armament limitation were agreed, it could be supervised. This still leaves the possibility of 11, a global war fought with limited weapons. Fearful as this would be, it does not arouse the horror that the thought of unlimited war does.

I find it extremely difficult to follow the train of thought of those who believe that this would be possible. The object of supervision, inspection, and control (international ownership being at present dropped out of consideration altogether), would be to prevent a sudden, all-out attack in peacetime; and admittedly for that purpose some form of supervision would probably be effective. So that as long as we distrust one another sufficiently to believe such an attack to be possible, it is worth continuing to think how best each country can demonstrate its good faith. As I said before, I believe that a mixing of scientists and engineers would be one good way. It would not, however, guard against atomic installations set up in distant territories and not openly declared. That I must talk about later.

What does seem to me to be quite certain is that once war had broken out between countries which were capable of making major weapons, nothing could stop their doing just that. International controls could not continue to work inside warring nations. Foreigners would be interned or sent home. Not only rigged bombs but other weapons of mass destruction could be made within a year or two. Agreements, or fear of retaliation might operate to prevent their use for a time. But if we suspect one another *now* of being morally capable of making a surprise attack with atomic weapons without a declaration of war, surely it is even more certain that such an attack would sooner or later be made when a global war was actually raging? It does seem to me to be much more impractical and unrealistic to suppose that, in the race that would follow, the warring nation that could first make a hydrogen bomb would not at once use it. Suspicion would certainly run very high. Morality is at a very low level in wartime, and it would be no more difficult to rationalize the use of one hydrogen bomb to end a holocaust than it was to rationalize the dropping of the first atomic bomb on Hiroshima to end World War II.

Those who agree with this argument seem to think that it will put an end to global war altogether, and that we need only contemplate minor wars in future. If so, it seems madness that just when we most need to conserve our world resources of scientific and technical ability to deal with the problems of a rapidly increasing world population that is determined to maintain or improve its standard of living, we in the West, and here I include the USSR together with the USA and Great Britain, are now exploding in nuclear tests, in this year in which I write, A.D. 1956, about fifty times the equivalent of all the TNT that was dropped on Germany throughout the whole of World War II!

When shall we feel safe enough to stop weapon development if we do not stop it now? Is a 20-megaton rigged bomb not big enough? One of the reasons given for further tests (I nearly wrote 'excuses', but I am trying to be as reasonable as possible myself) was the need to try out defence measures. Do we then contemplate global war I seriously and if so, is Great Britain just written off? For while the USA and the USSR might conceivably survive an all-out war in a twisted mangled form, Britain would not. To suppose that she would is to shut one's eyes to all the facts.

Some time, of course, we *must* stop these tests. If they continue and if other nations begin to join in, so that they continue at an accelerated rate, then by George Orwell's 1984 we, or rather our children, may have absorbed really dangerous doses of fallout, considerably more than what the medical authorities call the 'maximum permissible dose'. But when we do have the sense to stop, we shall have to try to persuade other nations to forgo their right also to contaminate international waters or stretches of desert land as we have done. That may in itself be difficult if we contemplate possibility III, minor wars fought with small atomic weapons.

We have been told recently, time and time again, that atomic warfare has become conventional; that to eliminate atomic weapons would cripple the forces of SEATO or NATO, that all sections of the armed forces will use them; and that small atomic bombs, atomic shells, and of course atomic-powered submarines will certainly be used by the nations that have them, in any future war. Many people advocated their use in Korea. It has been rightly pointed out that because they were not used in Korea, or in Indochina, the result was stalemate, or an effective defeat of the Western powers involved.

If atomic weapons of any kind were used by the Great Powers on each other, that would precipitate a global war, and a global war of type I. We can hardly suppose that a nation attacked with small atomic bombs would not retaliate with bombs of as large a size as they or their allies possessed. If small atomic bombs were used on us, would we surrender at once? Would we, in fact, have any choice, since we have permitted the USA to establish bombing bases on British soil?

What many people do contemplate is that while we should avoid using atomic weapons against any nation that has them to use back, we should be free to use them on nations that do not have them, such as Egypt and the People's Republic of China. If that is our intention, or our threat, or if we are even suspected of being likely to do this, then we must indeed expect that those other nations will build up their own atomic strength if and when they can. It will take time, but perhaps not more time than our children's or grandchildren's lifetime. Are you happy about that? I am not.

If that is not our intention, then to talk of using atomic weapons as part of conventional warfare is bluff. But it is most dangerous bluff, for it adds to the general feeling of fear, suspicion, and insecurity in the world, and these in themselves are powerful causes of war. I feel it difficult to believe that those practical men and women who support this kind of behaviour have seriously considered the consequences of it, and are not, in a sense, living politically from hand to mouth.

Unless I am mistaken, what they really hope for is that a demonstration of material strength will keep the Great Powers from flying at each other for long enough either for the particular economic and political system they dislike (communism or capitalism, as the case may be) to disintegrate, or for the two to find some *modus vivendi,* some way of living together peaceably, if not co-operatively, as England and Scotland, or Britain and Eire have done, up to a point.

Those who think like this clearly skate on thin ice as far as the rest of the world is concerned. For as long as the Great Powers are still divided, and highly armed into the bargain, there is always the danger that they may fine up on each side in a dispute between one of them and any other nation, or between two or more other nations. The biggest danger, I firmly believe, is from statesmen or generals who were cavalry officers in their younger days, or who have been educated at old-time military establishments and who still instinctively think first in terms of military solutions to political or economic or social problems. To them, atomic weapons are just one more tool.

To wait for the disintegration or metamorphosis of the political system one dislikes may mean waiting a very long time.

In the meantime one obvious danger is that there is a sense of moral superiority that accompanies the dislike of another political system. It may be justified. But if it takes the form of supposing that one's own nation is charged with the task of acting as the world's policeman, judge, and executioner, in the absence of any adequate world court of justice, then it becomes dangerous indeed. Because it seems as if this sense of moral superiority can completely blind a nation to the wickedness of the methods employed.

Many people believe that the Korean war was such a police action, undertaken by the USA in the first place and then by Britain and some other members of the UN, to uphold the interests of law and order. I doubt whether our more civilized descendants, looking back without passion at that episode, so discreditable to both sides, would recognize a legitimate police method in the use of napalm: liquid fire. We used it; and we call ourselves a Christian nation.

CHAPTER 8

The whole problem of international law and order is one that must be faced squarely by any would-be-realistic pacifist. But not only by the pacifist. The non-pacifist who wants to reduce war to a minimum (and who does not?) must face it too, and in the new context of the nuclear age.

Who are the criminals? What laws do they break? By whom should they be apprehended? And how? Before what court could they be brought and who shall judge them? How are they to be punished? And how can the punishment be confined to those who are really guilty?

I am quite unqualified to discuss this question from a legal point of view, nor do I think that that is what is wanted. Legal systems differ in different countries and although a vast body of international law exists and legal methods of deciding between international litigants are available, none of them are capable of dealing with situations like Korea or Formosa or, indeed, with a Hitler. In the case of the Suez Canal they were not tried.

The judgements of Tokyo and Nuremberg, however little we may sympathize with the defendants, were those of the victors judging the vanquished. The superficiality of the procedure has been manifested by the way in which many of these judgements have been quietly forgotten, or sentences drastically abridged in recent years, when the rearmament of Japan and Germany became 'desirable' once more.

How far does military victory bestow an internationally legal title, and after what length of time? How morally binding are settlements or treaties made as the result of force; made either under duress or between victors dividing the spoils of war? Civil contracts of this type would hardly be legally tolerated: a will made under 'undue influence' is not valid; still less a division of the swag by armed robbers. When I visited China in 1955 feeling about Formosa was running high and I heard many arguments to the effect that past legal treaties had declared that Formosa was part of China and that clearly they, the people on the mainland, *were* China. I remain unconvinced that any treaty or court, however constituted, had the right to hand over not only a territory, but a *body of people* from one government to another. Still less, however, can I see that war confers any such right. Might is not right.

It is not easy to clear one's mind (or at least it is not easy to the non-lawyer) as to the difference between law and morality, especially where the law has not been codified. It would appear that those who make or administer the law attempt to express and to maintain certain fundamental principles of justice, commonly agreed. But national laws can only be effective when the majority of citizens are naturally law-abiding. So it would seem that international law can only be really dynamic when it is the accepted expression of the intention of at least some governments to act justly, no matter what others may do.

It might have been supposed that the legality or otherwise of the use of certain kinds of weapons, or of experimentation with them, that involves not only the contamination of international waters and of the world's atmosphere but also injustice or danger to innocent inhabitants of Trust Territories, would be matters that should long ago have been referred to an unbiased International Court of Justice. It is clear, however, that this opinion is not accepted by those nations that are stockpiling nuclear weapons and who regard themselves as the custodians of the world's peace and security. But does justice allow a man to be judge in his own cause?

If we look back for a moment into the past, we find that many people have been deeply concerned about the question of the formulation and enforcement of international law. The Society of Friends itself came into being about the time when the idea of the 'Law of Nations' was beginning to influence the thinking of politicians, following the publication by Hugo Grotius of his great work *On the Law of War and Peace*. Part of his preface might well be quoted in connexion with what I have already written:

I, for the reasons which I have stated, holding it to be most certain that there is among nations a common Law of Rights which is of force with regard to war, and in war, saw many and grave causes why I should write a book on that subject. For I saw prevailing throughout the Christian world a licence of making war of which even barbarous nations would have been ashamed; recourse being had to arms for slight reasons or no reason; and when arms were once taken up, all reverence for divine and human law was thrown away, just as if men were thenceforth authorized to commit all crimes without restraint.

Since Grotius's time, peace treaties have been formulated as legal documents and statesmen have at least tried to justify their actions in legal terms. For instance, they always classify expenditure, even on hydrogen bombs, as 'military defence'.

One early Friend, William Penn, had a legal training that stood him in good stead in 1670, when the judge attempted to intimidate the jury that was trying him at the Old Bailey (the case that is known to jurists as the Bushell case, after the brave foreman of the jury in question). In 1693, after his retirement from being the first governor of Pennsylvania, he wrote *An Essay Towards the Present and Future Peace of Europe*[9] in which, in legal terms, he proposed a Parliament of Europe with ninety representatives from all the European Nations including 'the Turks and Muscovites'. This was to meet in a round room with many doors, so that there might be no quarrels over precedence. How well he knew his men!

His system had one improvement (within its own limitations) over our present United Nations, and that was that *every* (European) sovereign power had to be represented, and was to be present, under heavy penalties, throughout the whole of each session. There was to be no picking and choosing of mem-

9 Now published as a pamphlet by the Society of Friends Peace Committee, Euston Road, London, England.

bers and no evading of responsibilities. One of the great advantages of such a Parliament of Europe he believed to be the personal friendships that would be formed by personal contact. 'For princes have the curiosity of seeing the courts and cities of other countries, as well as private men.... It was a great motive to the tranquillity of the world that they could freely converse face to face, and personally and reciprocally give and receive marks of civility and kindness.'

I think we still might learn something from William Penn: 'Force may subdue,' he wrote, 'but love gains.... Nor would the worst of men easily be brought to hurt those that they really think love them. It is that love and patience must in the end have the victory.... Love is the hardest lesson in Christianity; but for that reason it should be most our care to learn it. *Difficilia quae pulchra.*' And he had had some experience, too, in his lifetime, in prison and out of it.

In the latter part of the nineteenth century Peace Societies in general concentrated their study a good deal on the possibilities of establishing a *Court of the Nations* for the settlement of all disputes by arbitration and other forms of judicial procedure. A series of conferences on peace and arbitration was held between 1895 and 1916 at which Friends found the greatest difficulty in coming to any agreement on the problem of *sanctions.*[10]Law can only work when it is protected and, if necessary, enforced on the law-breaker who must be either prevented in time before, or punished after, the commitment of a crime. Prevention and punishment imply the element of coercive force. If a nation, represented by its government, breaks the law, e.g. by resorting to aggression, the use of coercive force against such a collective body is equal to war, even if it is embellished by the name of 'police action'. The dilemma of the pacifist lawyer, then, is that he wants to replace the arbitrary violence of war by the rational method of justice, but finds himself back at the necessity of war just along that way.

10 Margaret E. Hirst *The Quakers in Peace and War*, p. 448 Swarthmore Press (now Geo. Allen & Unwin, London), 1923.

The same question of sanctions as applied to delinquent nations was discussed by the Friends World Conference of 1937 at its commission on international justice, which finally agreed to disagree.

An agreement to disagree obviously leaves us more or less where we were. What is clear is that the problem itself is not a new one, either for statesmen or for pacifists. What *is* new is the fact that the invention of modern scientific weapons has placed enormous destructive power in the hands of all nations (actually or potentially) whether they are the policeman or the criminal.

First the League of Nations and then the United Nations have tried to deal with the problem of a so-called criminal nation by a system of collective security. Chapter VII of the UN Charter gives detailed provisions for the use of military sanctions, including 'actions by air, sea and land forces'. There seem to be a number of practical, as distinct from moral, objections to this type of international action; and these would apply equally to any system of World Government that might supplement or supersede the United Nations.

The first difficulty is that of deciding which party or nation is the real criminal, and the second is that of finding an unbiased judge or jury. Attempts have been made in recent years to define 'aggression'. The Soviet Union proposed a draft definition to the United Nations in 1950. This immediately provoked a reaction against their definition or any other, because at the time many members of the United Nations felt that the USSR was a conspiracy of criminals anyhow. One comment made a little later was that the most radical of Western statesmen 'would even doubt that two times two equals four, if it happens to be a communist who says so'.

Looking back at the Soviet draft after an interval of some six years, it seems as if it might have been at least an honest attempt to obtain agreement on what constitutes 'aggression' that would prevent errors on the one hand and hasty judgements on the other. If we all condemn aggressors but disagree as to what aggression is, the only possible procedure is that each incident has to be judged on its merits. And this is just what many States have argued ought to be done. The arguments have been admirably set out by the distinguished physicist, Dr Hans Thirring, in an article in the *Bulletin of the Atomic Scientists*.[11] Some members of the UN thought that what constituted aggression was not the degree or kind of violence that had occurred, but the aggressive *intention*. That could only be judged by the circumstances in the particular case. Others argued that if a list of aggressive acts were enumerated then a potential aggressor would find some way of acting aggressively that was not covered by the list and so could evade condemnation. Income tax regulations are continually trying to catch up with legal evasions!

A third argument was that the list did not cover *internal aggression*: the encouragement and financial support of a 'fifth column' in another State, or of any subversive movements trying to overthrow the régime of that State. A Netherlands delegate pointedly remarked that 'A country wishing to engage in internal aggression would naturally want any resort to armed force in self-defense against it to be forbidden.' If internal aggression so defined may legitimately be resisted by armed force in self-defence, how are we to define the official foreign policy of the USA, approved by Great Britain, which was described by John Foster Dulles at a press conference at Denver on 8 August 1952, in these words:

We will abandon the policy of mere containment, and will actively develop hope and a resistance spirit within the captive peoples which, in my opinion, is the only alternative to general war.

The judge, or policeman, who copies the crime that he condemns, hardly demonstrates his fitness for his self-appointed post. Of course it might, and would be claimed that one subversive movement is aiming at the overthrow of a *good* (that is, a democratic) government, whereas the other encourages the overthrow of a *bad* (that is, a communist) government. But the communist claims to be the only *good* democrat, and accuses the Western governments of being capitalist and therefore *bad*. We are in the fantastic position

11 Chicago, April 1953.

of having two parties, each claiming to be the policeman-judge-executioner and each accusing the other of being the criminal.

If it is argued that this is a matter to be decided by the United Nations as a whole, it can equally, and with much justice, be argued that the United Nations Organization is neither representative nor impartial. As long as the five or six hundred million inhabitants of China are 'represented' only by a former government which originally imposed itself by force, which was deposed by force and which has not the slightest chance of being reinstated; while the Latin-American states, most of which are heavily dependent on the USA, each have an individual vote, what kind of jury can we expect the UN to be? Where the interests of the great powers are not concerned, it is capable of functioning relatively impartially; it may sometimes even act as a brake upon the great powers; it has certainly attempted to do so; and it has frequently functioned well as a negotiator; but as a jury and judge it has a chequered record.

However that may be, any realist must admit that, unless the USSR and the USA agree, any attempt on the part of either to 'discipline' another nation could develop into a major war. Even if they were to agree, it is only as long as they have a monopoly – not a majority but a monopoly – of nuclear weapons, that they would be able to force their united will on other nations without fear of retaliation, and then only, in the last resort, by mass murder.

The really hopeful factor in the modern situation is that irrespective of the question of punishment, nations do nowadays attempt to justify their behaviour in quasi-legal terms. They try to prove that they were being attacked, or might have been attacked, and therefore were exercising their 'inherent rights of individual or collective self-defence'. They argue, as the Soviet Union has done in respect of Hungary, or France in respect of Algeria, or South Africa in respect of 'apartheid', that their behaviour was a matter of internal policy only and not subject to international judgement or scrutiny. They argue that they were attempting to protect their own nationals on foreign soil and were therefore not aggressors in the generally accepted sense of the word. Or they argue that their action was necessary in order to rectify a longstanding injustice. And this kind of appeal to world opinion comes from both sides, as it has done time and time again in the Israel-Arab dispute, or in the Suez Canal controversy, and as it did in the Korean war.

The fact that there can be such an appeal to world opinion, as well as the attempt on the part even of a dictatorial government to justify itself to its own people, means that nations do recognize the moral force of law, even when they resort to armed violence. Setting aside for the time being the case of the 'mad dog aggressor', it would seem that far more conflicts might be settled by an appeal to justice, if it were clear that a decision would be made on the basis of obvious justice and not on a basis of prejudice, expediency, favouritism, or self-interest. This surely means that any International Court of Justice which is to decide disputes between mutually accusing nations, or which is to decide whether a nation is guilty or not guilty of a crime, must be administered by men who are not representatives of nations or swayed by national interests. The United Nations Security Council and General Assembly, both of which are composed of delegates who cannot be regarded as impartial, simply do not fill the bill. The World Court of Justice could do so if the more powerful nations referred more to it and respected its judgements, not only on minor issues, as now, but also on major ones, where they stand to lose substantially, either financially or in prestige.

At present the more powerful nations, of which ours is still one, are often able to sway a decision in the UN or in other negotiations, not through their obvious integrity, but because of their economic or military superiority. We boast of it. That is precisely what 'Negotiation from strength' means. Nevertheless it is becoming increasingly clear that conflicts ought to be settled by reason on the basis of justice, and not by force. We are being driven to this conclusion by the suicidal nature of modern war, but the fact is true irrespective of the quality of the force involved.

The real difficulty, it seems to me, is that many of the disputes between nations are based on enmities which are deep-seated and long-standing, with acts of violence on both sides, and often with real grievances on both sides. So that, as an Irish Friend has written to me of the Irish problem, 'However it may seem to the Almighty, humanly speaking there is no solution free of substantial injustice . . . if you ask how the course of history might have been different and better it is difficult to give a convincing answer.' He goes on to say of this particular question: 'The problem is perhaps fairly described as the effect on the soul of a small and unsuccessful nation forced by geography to live next to a wealthy and successful neighbour. But beyond that there are difficult questions of the difference between the Celt and the Anglo-Saxon, which is very great, and not entirely (I think) the consequence of their environment.'

A World Court of Justice which had to operate in a world where many nations had hydrogen bombs, or were capable of making them, would simply not be able to use violence to enforce its judgements. However unpalatable that may be to men used to thinking in old grooves, it must be accepted. If I were an Old Testament prophet, I might express this in terms of God's judgement on violence, that ultimately it either destroys itself or destroys those who use it. I am more concerned that an alternative to violence, a just alternative, shall be built up to replace it, in time to prevent world suicide. At the same time I am sure that we shall have to recognize that just as in ordinary human relationships there are crimes with which the law cannot deal, or with which it cannot deal without injustice ('Hard cases make bad law', we say), so also there will be national or international crimes which no human law, international or national, can *punish,* except in terms of an expression of abhorrence; and international disputes for which there is no entirely just and reasonable solution. The plain statement that this is so might go a long way to assuage bad feelings, and to induce the nations concerned to find a compromise for themselves.

CHAPTER 9

Perhaps there is no international dispute which so well illustrates the problem of finding *any* just and reasonable solution whatever, as that which now exists between Israel and the Arab States.

The Jews, persecuted in one country after another, had never ceased to regard themselves as a 'people', or Palestine as their home. But it was a home which had belonged to others for nearly two thousand years, even though some Jews had always lived there. For the past one thousand years or more, the Moslems had not only recognized the right of Christians to visit Palestine as pilgrims, but the right of Jews to come and live there as permanent settlers. They lived under Mohammedan rule, and it was not much easier for them there than in many of the other countries in which they settled; but they could come.

The idea of national self-determination is of Western origin: it took root among the Arabs and among the Jews almost at the same time. The modern Jewish nationalist movement stemmed from a period of intense persecution in the latter part of the nineteenth century; it seized the opportunity of the first World War to establish, in the eyes of the world, the right of the Jewish people to make for themselves a National Home in Palestine; and then, when a fresh blast of persecution assailed them before and during the second World War, Jews felt compelled to consolidate their position and to press for the immediate establishment of Palestine as a Jewish State, in order to have the right to control immigration themselves. They regard their right to Palestine as based on religion, on history, and on various legal documents, finally confirmed by the 1947 Partition decision of the United Nations. In addition they can point out that they purchased or rented much of the land and that they farm it more efficiently than the Arabs ever did. Apart from the passage of time, they have more legal right to it, perhaps, than the Americans have to America, or the Australians to Australia. But their principal attachment to Palestine is a mystical one.

In saying this, one ignores the fact that the Arabs were there and that although for four hundred years the Arabs have been subject to Turkish domination, an Arab nationalist movement, based partly on Western ideas of democracy and partly on the revolt against Turkish misrule, had been growing in power. A great Jewish thinker, Ahad Ha'am, warned his compatriots, and especially the ardent Zionists in the 1890s, that they must not ignore the Arabs. These were his words:

> How careful must we be in dealing with an alien people in whose midst we want to settle. How essential it is to practise kindness and esteem towards them. . . . For if ever the Arab could consider the action of his rivals to be oppression or the robbing of his rights then, even if he keeps silent and waits for his time to come, the rage will remain alive in his heart.[12]

Nearly thirty years later Ahad Ha'am expressed his bitter disappointment at the course of events in the words 'since the beginning of the Palestinian colonization we have always considered the Arab people as non-existent'.

Britain's record in this dispute is not particularly creditable, although there was plenty of idealism to begin with. The mistakes we have made have been due partly to the incorrigible tendency we share with other nations to play power politics in order to protect our national interests, partly to stupidity and exasperation and not, as is sometimes suggested, to deliberate wickedness or irresponsibility.

12 Quoted by Dr Walter Zander in a moving pamphlet *Is this the Way? A Call to Jews*, published by Gollancz Ltd, London, 1948.

By 1914, the great Ottoman Empire was already collapsing; the first World War only completed a process that had begun many years earlier. Rich provinces had been surrendered to Russia, who also wanted Constantinople and the Straits. France had Tunisia and claimed Syria. Cyprus, long a prey to one powerful neighbour after another, had been ruled by the Turks for 200 years, but in 1878 Great Britain took over the administration in consideration of a payment of £92,800 a year to the Sultan of Turkey, who retained nominal sovereignty. In 1914, Great Britain assumed complete rights over the island, and although in 1915 she offered to cede it to Greece in return for aid to Serbia, the offer was refused, and Cyprus remained a British possession. In spite of increased prosperity under British administration, there is a strong movement for self-determination among the Cypriots, most of whom are of Greek origin, and whose discontent has been fanned, to put it mildly, by the Greek Orthodox Church. But as long as Britain envisages conditions in the Middle East in which British interests are being or might be threatened, Cyprus is said to be too valuable a military base to be released.

Egypt had also been part of the Ottoman Empire, but in 1882 British forces entered, at the request of the Khedive (Viceroy), to suppress an internal rising, and there they stayed. Again the suzerainty of the Sultan of Turkey was recognized, but Britain had effective control, and during the first World War, her occupation was converted into a protectorate. Without consulting the Egyptian people, by Article 152 of the 1919 Peace Treaty the name of Britain was substituted for that of the Imperial Ottoman Empire in the Suez Canal Convention of 1888, so giving an appearance of legality to the Guardianship of the Canal by Britain. In 1922, Egypt was proclaimed an independent sovereign state and the British protectorate ended, but British troops remained in Egypt, though not with the willing consent of the Egyptian government.

In 1924, Egypt proposed that British troops should be withdrawn and that protection of the international character of the Suez Canal should be entrusted to the League of Nations. Britain refused. The Anglo-Egyptian Treaty of 1936, which was concluded under stress of the Fascist threat in North Africa, did give Britain the legal right to maintain forces in the Canal Zone for a period of 20 years, but in 1952 Egypt renounced the Treaty unilaterally, and she also refused to become an equal partner in the Baghdad Pact, which would have meant that she was still obliged to have foreign troops in her country. In the summer of 1956 British troops finally evacuated the Canal Zone in fulfilment of the 1936 Treaty obligations, and shortly afterwards the Egyptian President announced the nationalization of the Suez Canal Company. The fact that Egypt had already, in defiance of the United Nations, closed the Canal to Israeli shipping, has been explained by President Nasser as a result of the fact that Egypt regarded herself as being still at war with Israel, whose frontier, in fact, she frequently raided. Britain had similarly closed the Canal to Axis shipping during World War II, and at the time of writing, has attacked Egypt in the face of widespread international disapproval, but has withdrawn her troops once more.

Going back to the first World War, one can see how, in spite of the habit of regarding peace treaties as an opportunity for the victors to bargain on the division of the spoils, new ideas concerning international obligations had then begun to spread, though mixed up with the old power politics. The British High Commissioner in Cairo, Sir Henry McMahon, had on 24 October 1915 sent a letter to the Sherif Hussein, Arab ruler of Mecca, who was regarded by the British as able to win Arab sympathy for the Allies. In this letter he had promised that Arab independence would be recognized for all lands inhabited by Arabic-speaking peoples, with certain exceptions. He supposed that he had made it quite clear that Palestine, in which France also had an interest, was to be one such exception, but in fact, owing to bad drafting, the wording was not clear at all; and the Sherif Hussein, who had published the Arabic text of the letter straight away, certainly allowed the Arabs to suppose that they had been promised independence for Palestine. The British had not only thought that the letter was clear, but they had also regarded the correspondence as confidential and for some time they neither published the English text, nor gave any interpretation of it.

They certainly did not intend the Balfour Declaration of November 1917 to be a piece of double-dealing. In fact they were very careful indeed about the exact wording, which read:

> His Majesty's Government view with favour the establishment in Palestine of a national home for the Jewish people, and will use their best endeavours to facilitate the achievement of this object, it being clearly understood that nothing shall be done which may prejudice the civil and religious rights of existing non-Jewish communities in Palestine or the rights and political status enjoyed by Jews in any other country.

What Dr Weizmann and other Jewish negotiators had asked for was much more than this. They had asked for the 're-establishment of Palestine as the Jewish National Home'. The British Government, by promising only to promote 'the establishment in Palestine of a national home for the Jewish people', and by making it clear that they refused to prejudice the rights of the non-Jewish inhabitants, also supposed that they had clearly refused to support the claim of the Jews to absolute rule over the country. When, at the beginning of 1918, the Sherif Hussein heard about the Balfour Declaration, he was assured by a spokesman of the British Foreign Office that 'the economic and political freedom of the Arab population' in Palestine would be safeguarded. How 'civil and religious rights' became changed into 'economic and political freedom' is not quite clear; perhaps the British thought they were the same thing.

One of President Wilson's famous fourteen points stated that 'Turkish portions of the present Ottoman empire should be assured a secure sovereignty, but the other nationalities which are now under Turkish rule should be assured undoubted security of life, and an absolutely unmolested opportunity of autonomous development'. This again gave the Arabs cause to believe that they would achieve full independence at once, but they did not. Article 22 of the Covenant of the League of Nations stated that 'to territories which are inhabited by peoples not yet able to stand by themselves under the strenu-

ous conditions of the modern world there should be applied the principle
that the wellbeing and the development of such peoples form a sacred trust
of civilization'. It specifically named 'certain communities, formerly belonging
to the Turkish Empire' as having 'reached a stage of development where their
existence as independent nations can be provisionally recognized, subject to
the rendering of administrative advice and assistance by a mandatary until
such times as they are able to stand alone'. It also, however, stated that 'the
wishes of these communities must be a principal consideration in the selection of the mandatary'.

The Arabs did not see the need for any mandate. If there had to be a
mandatory power they would have preferred it to be the USA. They felt
that their wishes had been overruled by the interests of Britain and France.
They saw in the British encouragement to the Jewish people to settle in
Palestine, which was put under a British mandate, a direct violation of
what they had regarded as a promise that Palestine should be theirs. In
April 1920, the Arabs in Jerusalem rioted; and the Holy Land, holy to Jews,
Christians, and Moslems alike, has been the scene of hatred and intermit-
tent bloodshed ever since.

At first the Jewish influx into Palestine was small. As lately as 1932, Dr
Weizmann publicly disowned any claim for the establishment of a Jewish
State there. But as the Nazi regime rose to power in Germany, so the situation
of the Jews in Central Europe became more desperate. Many of them looked
to Palestine as their only hope and masses of immigrants began to pour in.
The Arab revolt that followed took the British three years to subdue, and
the justice of the Arab case, or the need to mollify the Arab world, led to
the issue, in May 1939, of the White Paper which permitted the admission
of another 74,000 Jews but made further immigration dependent upon
Arab consent. The Peel Commission of 1936 had described the Palestine
disturbances as 'fundamentally a conflict of right with right', 'the outcome
of a conflict between Arab and Jewish nationalism', but whereas the Arab
nationalism felt frustrated, the Jewish nationalism was developing under the
pressure of Nazi persecution but also under British protection.

The White Paper of 1939, followed by the outbreak of World War II three months later, changed the situation entirely. Restrictions on immigration just at the very time when large-scale Jewish immigration had become most urgent seemed intolerable to the Jews. It was regarded by them as appeasement by Britain of the Arabs, of a peculiarly loathsome kind. It is described, more charitably, by Dr Zander as 'only a very imperfect, heavy-handed, clumsy attempt to deal with a situation which itself had become unbearable'. There was increasing pressure from the USA upon Britain, as mandatory power, to permit much larger numbers of Jewish immigrants into Palestine. The USA itself was not prepared to admit indefinite numbers of Jewish refugees into America. A Jewish Conference held at Biltmore, USA, in 1942 demanded that Palestine should be made a Jewish Commonwealth, and that unlimited Jewish immigration should be permitted, under Jewish auspices.

Faced with pressure from the USA and the enmity of both Jews and Arabs, Britain offered to allow the admission of 96,000 immigrants over a period of two years, the decision on further immigration to be left to the High Commissioner. This offer was refused both by the Jews, who wanted more, and by the Arabs, who found it too much. So Britain threw in her hand, and in February 1947, announced her intention of relinquishing the mandate.

On 29 November 1947, the United Nations General Assembly decided on a scheme of partition, which was implemented later, when part of Palestine became a Jewish State, and parts remained under Arab control. For this UN decision a two-thirds majority was required. In fact 33 nations voted for partition, 13 against it. It seemed a big majority, but it would be wrong to interpret this as meaning that world opinion was heavily in favour of the justness of the Jewish cause.

The thirty-three states in favour of the Jewish state have a total population of about 560 million, against 480 million of those who voted against it. But if one considers that the eleven nations who did not vote at all represent no less than 625 million people, it appears that out of the total populations represented in the General Assembly only 33.6 per cent voted for partition, whilst 37.5 per cent abstained and 28.9 per cent opposed it: and the proportion of those in favour becomes probably even smaller if it is taken into account that more than 400 million people (including the people of North Africa, Burma, Manchuria, Indonesia and Japan) were not represented at all.

Infinitely more important, however, is the composition of the character of the two groups. The neighbours of the new Jewish state, without any exception – reaching from Egypt to Iraq and beyond to India, and from Greece and Turkey to Saudi Arabia – were united in their opposition, whilst most of those who declared themselves for the Jewish state are far removed from the scene of action. Many of them have only a small real interest in the matter themselves, and some of them could be induced to change their opinion from one day to the other, whilst the Arabs and their supporters feel strongly in the matter, and most of them consider the issue as their own.

But even more significant than the political issue is the fact that many of those who opposed partition are sincerely convinced that the legal and moral right is on their side and that the establishment of the Jewish state under the existing conditions is a breach of law and a violation of the established principles of national freedom and personality.[13]

This was written in December 1947. Under the Partition Scheme the area of Israel was to be 5,687 square miles, but fighting broke out in May 1948, during the confusion which followed the abrupt withdrawal of Britain from its position as mandatory authority. The Jews had access to supplies of arms and were united, the Arabs were not, in spite of the existence of the Arab League, formed in March 1945. The tendency towards Arabic co-operation and unity has been opposed by unwillingness on the part of the existing Arab States to surrender to any central authority the control of their individual affairs and especially of their foreign policies. The result of the Palestine War was a succession of major setbacks for the Arabs, an increase of Israel territory to 7,800 square miles, and the creation of a huge refugee problem. According to the basic statistics of the UN Relief and Works Agency (UNRWA), there were in June 1956 a total of 922,279 Arab refugees from Palestine officially

13 Dr Zander, *loc. cit.*

recognized by UNRWA and in receipt of rations, of whom about 102,600 live in the Lebanon, 90,000 in Syria, 512,700 in Jordan, and 17,000 in the Gaza district. Apart from these there are a few thousands in Iraq and in Egypt; and many thousands of others in West Jordan and Gaza who do not qualify for rations but are in desperate need.

The gravity of the situation may be seen by the fact that in the Gaza district, for example, only about 40,000 of the 300,000 inhabitants are self-supporting, and there are 221 refugees to every 100 original residents. The birth-rate among the refugees is high, so that their number is increasing by some 25,000 (about 3 per cent) every year. The United Nations General Assembly has expressed the view that those refugees who wish to do so should be allowed to return to their homes. Under intense pressure, Israel agreed in 1949 to the repatriation of not more than 100,000 with a maximum of 250,000 refugees in Israel altogether. These would return not necessarily to their former homes, many of which were destroyed, but to areas determined by Israel herself, in accordance with her own economic and security needs. The Arabs have rejected this offer completely. They claim that all refugees should be the responsibility of Israel. The Israeli offer has therefore been withdrawn. The Jews, with their own history so vivid in their memories, are not unsympathetic towards these unhappy refugees; they are willing to help them generously and to receive back some of them who wish to be reunited with their families. But as long as Israel is virtually surrounded by enemies, and her frontiers subject to constant attack; bearing in mind that many of the refugees themselves have learned (or been taught) to hate the Jews because they regard them as the cause of all their troubles; bearing in mind also that Israel is largely a nation of refugees, and is still in grave economic and psychological difficulties; the Israeli government naturally feels that they cannot undertake to absorb a minority of nearly one million dissident and needy people.

Nor are the Arab States willing to absorb them. They do not recognize the very existence of Israel as a State. They insist that absolute justice requires the return of the refugees to their former homeland. They have been ready to wait, indefinitely if need be, for the economic collapse of Israel; and by constant frontier enmity to demonstrate that their resentment still lives. Israel, fearing the supply of Soviet arms to Egypt, and seizing the opportunity afforded by the Suez Canal dispute, has now attacked, followed by the British and French, and for the time being the result is a stalemate.

Although there are close bands of racial kinship between the Jews and the Arabs, Israel is in Arab and, to a certain extent in Asian, eyes a protege of the West, and as such was not invited to the Asian-African Bandung Conference of 1955.

But the Jews in Israel do not regard their nation as a protege of anybody, even though the political sympathies of many would be with the West. They believe themselves to be a people uniquely chosen by God to fulfil His purpose. They are used to isolation. They see in their return to Palestine the culmination of two thousand years of wandering and suffering, and they look to the future with a Messianic expectation. Yet they are also a secular state, and their government is a military one, which thinks in terms of massive military reprisals.

Where, in such a situation, is absolute justice to be found? Justice cannot be built upon a foundation of violence, counter-violence, and resentment. The Arabs had urged that the legality of the decision about partition should be referred to the World Court of Justice. The United Nations had refused this demand, which questions the right of the General Assembly to make binding decisions. The task of the United Nations in attempting to supervise the change-over from the mandatary to the partition regime was made much harder by the refusal of Great Britain to allow the UN supervisory committee to land before 1 May 1948, and by the condition of administrative chaos in which Palestine was left when Britain withdrew on 15 May 1948, eight hours after the establishment of an Israeli government. On the very same day hostilities began.

The attempt by Britain, France, and America to prevent further Israel-Arab hostilities by the Tripartite Declaration of 1950 gained a slight breathing-space, but was essentially unrealistic in the context of the modern world, if looked at as a long-term policy. Probably it was not intended to be any such thing.

This Declaration had two aims: firstly, to keep the supply of arms to both sides at a low level; this was only possible as long as the West had a virtual monopoly of arms: secondly, to prevent a new outbreak of hostilities between Israel and the Arab States by immediate joint action of the Western Powers 'both within and without the United Nations'; this leaves the reactions of the USSR and of the Asian countries out of account, and has led to bitter differences within Britain herself, and in the United Nations, on the question of British intervention.

What *is* interesting about the Tripartite Declaration is its implied admissions: firstly, that hostilities are less likely to occur when national armaments are small – the very reverse of the 'peace through strength' policy that the Western Powers claim in respect of their own defences: secondly, that the prevention of an outbreak of hostilities is of even more importance than the assessment of responsibility for such an outbreak. In other words, their instinctive reaction is that of a mother who finds two of her children fighting: 'I don't care which of you began it. You must both stop it.'

The weakness of the usual argument that large armaments prevent war and that therefore the determination of Britain to have her own hydrogen bombs is a contribution to peace, is vividly shown up by the Israel-Arab dispute. Would we really feel that a flare-up in the Middle East would have been less likely if both the Jews and the Arabs had had nuclear weapons? Or are we again assuming that not only we in the West but the Soviet government also have such a monopoly of morality and common-sense that what applies to us does not apply to Jews and Arabs?

What about our taking a dose of the medicine that we prescribe for others?

CHAPTER 10

History teaches us that time can bring about reconciliations that seemed at another time impossible, but only when violence has ceased, whether by agreement or through exhaustion. The Israel-Arab dispute is essentially a matter of territorial sovereignty and, given time and absence of aggravation by other powers, such disputes seem to lose their urgency. This is not to say that a ruling by a genuinely objective and universally respected World Court of Justice would have no value at all. On the other hand, as long as national arms exist and as long as the more powerful states continue to play power politics, such a ruling might even be made the excuse for fresh hostilities. What does seem essential is that hostilities themselves and all their appendages, conscription, mobilization, military expenditure, should be recognized as the outstanding crime against humanity.

Crimes are sometimes committed by insane people. 'Mad-dog aggression' on the part of a mentally unsound nation could be argued to fall within this category. A favourite question put to young conscientious objectors by the members of Tribunals is 'How do you suppose that Hitler could have been dealt with except by war?' Any references to events earlier than 1936 are ruled out as being irrelevant and unrealistic. The question is: Once Nazi Germany was set on war, no matter what the mistakes (if any) were that brought about that situation, how could she have been prevented from pursuing a policy of aggression and aggrandizement except by warlike retaliation? Was not our mistake, in fact, that we did not recognize the situation soon enough, did not step up our own arms quickly enough to warn Hitler of certain defeat, and so were nearly defeated ourselves? It is a fair question, although not perhaps to a nervous and inexperienced lad who is expected to give an answer in a sentence or two about events that happened before he was born.

One answer could well be that a sufficient display of force might conceivably have stopped Hitler from further aggression at that time, but would hardly have rescued the Jews, the communists, and the pacifists from the concentration and extermination camps, nor eradicated the war spirit in Germany. Nearer to our own time, the American atomic bombs did not bring Soviet political prisoners back from Siberia nor repatriate German prisoners of war even after eight years. Not until the USSR had atomic and hydrogen bombs of her own and Stalin had died did the cold war ease up a little; and Dr Peter Kapitza, arrested and disgraced some years previously for his refusal to do nuclear weapons research, was reinstated in his job as Director of Moscow Institute for Physical Problems,[14] thus proving that there had been conscientious objectors even in Stalinist Russia.

The defeat and death of Hitler was certainly brought about by means of war, just as his rise was both due to and contributed to the mounting war psychosis in Germany. It was a war that killed not only Hitler but over 20 million men, women, and children with him in all the warring countries, that defeated Germany only to arm her again, that produced the first atomic weapons, that produced a refugee problem of enormous magnitude and that has reduced the economic strength of Britain so that she is gradually falling to the level of a second-rate power. It also sowed the seeds of the Palestinian and Korean Wars, and perhaps of future wars as well.

I do not know whether there could have been any cheaper way, politically speaking, of preventing Hitler from achieving his ambition to make Germany the master of the world. I doubt very much indeed whether any declaration on the part of a World Court of Justice would have stopped him. I doubt very much whether the possession of nuclear weapons by the Allied powers in, say, 1938, would have stopped him for longer than it would have taken German

14 *Science*, vol. 124 (1956), p. 361.

scientists and engineers to find out how to make them too; and I believe he would have used them if he had had them to use.

In other words, politically speaking, I am convinced that what happened or might have happened in 1939 is now completely irrelevant. It is completely irrelevant, that is, in the sense in which it is generally used, as an argument for universal conscription and other immense war preparations. If a mad-dog aggressor arises in a world of the future that is still armed, and armed with nuclear weapons, he can destroy that world and his own nation with it, and nothing can stop him except a miracle. God help us all if it happens. It could not happen in an unarmed world. An armed world breeds 'mad dogs'.

It is more likely, however, that if nuclear war comes in the future it will be not through aggression but through defence, not through frenzy but through fear. I see no hope whatever for a world that still regards war as a tool if used in a good cause, and not as a crime if used in any cause whatever. The real danger is not from dictators with a lust for power, dangerous as these may be in their time, but from the fact that both they and the more democratic governments can still rely on men and women who think of war as horrible but possible, men and women who have not learned to say 'No' to evil, to die rather than to kill, or to assist in community wrongdoing of any kind.

It seems to me, therefore, that the most effective answer that our young lad can give the members of the Tribunal is that Hitler would have had no power at all if German boys had not been willing to learn to kill, and that the Hitlers of the future will be able to destroy the world unless we learn to eliminate the means of making war: that we must educate men not to resort to war rather than train them for it. Such a change of heart can only come about, I firmly believe, if those who are convinced that war is wrong not only take no part in it – whether their individual refusal seems politically effective or not – but also join with others in removing the causes of war. They must join with others also in building up respect for an Impartial and objective World Court of Justice as a body to which all international disputes or grievances involving nations or governments can be referred. They must help others to learn how to meet aggression or oppression without submission and without violence.

I realize perfectly well that this is an immense programme, that it involves a revolution in our ways of thinking and behaviour, and that it will take time; and time is short. Those who believe in hydrogen bombs because they think they prevent war are, I believe, wrong. They clearly do not prevent minor wars, or internal revolts. We have had both. These weapons may indeed cause statesmen to hesitate and in that sense they may possibly have prevented Mr Dulles, for example, from falling over the brink to which he came several times. In that sense they may have prevented a major war, but no-one can say for certain. What is certain is that they are a morally wrong way of doing so. Morally wrong because they rely on fear instead of on justice, use threats instead of using understanding, provoke hatred instead of offering friendship, and misuse men, materials, and money that are needed to remove existing suffering, ignorance, and want.

Nevertheless, even if hydrogen bombs were the only way of preventing an immediate flare-up, those who believe in them ought still to be vitally concerned in promoting the revolution in our thinking and behaviour that will eliminate war itself. They should regard this not as a future ideal but as an immediate imperative. They ought to be seeking ways of educating young people all the world over to look upon war as a crime, if only because hydrogen bombs cannot keep the peace forever. If a nation has so lost its senses as to regard suicide as less to be feared than a fall in its standards of living, then it may risk war when its standards of living are threatened. And undoubtedly the standards of living of the richer powers will be threatened as the poorer nations gain in strength. There is simply not enough to go round for 5,000 million people to live at Western levels of comfort, even with the help of nuclear power. And the world population is not likely to be stabilized at a much lower figure; not within the next century or two, anyhow.

What many people seem chiefly concerned about at present, however, is not the elimination of the means of making war, not even the elimination of the grosser forms of human need, but the elimination of the particular form of government or of economic system that they dislike. Their motives are often mixed. They may persuade themselves that it is the existence of forced labour camps under communism or of the exploitation of colonial labour under capitalism that they abhor, whereas what they fear most may really be a treacherous attack on themselves and their country, or a lowering of their own standards of living. I have met Christian people in the USA who believe that communism was an invention of the devil. Curiously enough, in spite of their belief in God, they still felt that unless communism were attacked and eliminated, time was on the devil's side. I never could understand this twisted faith. But then I never could bring myself to believe in war as an instrument of God's purpose, or in communism as wholly evil. That those who believe in it had done evil things I had no doubt. So have we British.

Both in the Soviet Union and in China, however, and in other communist-governed countries I met other Christian people who, while not condoning the evil things done in their own countries, believed in communism as an effective and efficient political, social, and economic system with a high moral content. At the same time, partly no doubt as the result of propaganda, but partly because of the speeches of Western politicians, they were firmly convinced that the USA intended to attack them if there were the slightest chance of such an attack being made without retaliation.

What could a World Court of Justice say about such a dispute as this? Not very much, except as a matter of detail. If it were called upon to adjudicate upon the division of Germany, there could be little doubt that in justice the wishes of the people themselves, freely expressed, should be the proper factor in deciding their destiny; but would Britain then agree to a similar test being applied to Cyprus? Do the wishes of the Marshall Islanders get much of a hearing, where the interests of the USA and Britain are concerned?

The danger of war between the USA and the USSR seems to have receded, although it is never wholly absent as long as they are both armed. But each would rejoice to see the government of the other overthrown, or to see the overthrow of the influence that either has over other nations. Each fears the influx of spies or of saboteurs or agitators.

We are proud of the fact that our forefathers sailed to liberty in the *Mayflower*. Woe betide anyone who sails to liberty nowadays without a passport, a visa, or a permit. We often suppose this insularity to be peculiar to the USA (since not many people here would expect to find liberty anyhow in the USSR). It is true that it has been difficult for anyone except business-men and holidaymakers to get into or out of the USA. But it can be quite difficult to get into Britain too. A young American pacifist, a believer in the Gandhian principle of non-violent resistance to evil, a man who had served a prison sentence in the USA as a conscientious objector, recently decided to spend a month or so in Britain studying the various peace movements. It took him two and a half hours to convince the immigration officials that he was harmless. They found my name among his papers, which were thoroughly searched, but even that did not altogether reassure them! They probably thought he was a wolf in sheep's clothing, a communist travelling under false pretences. Although what a good government and a contented people should fear from communist agents I really fail to see.

Of course as long as military preparations exist there will be spies and secret agents. As long as rival forms of government exist there may be attempts on the part of each to undermine the other, especially if religious differences or economic interests are involved. There is, indeed, a steady gradation between the kind of persuasion or propaganda that could generally be accepted as mor-ally and legally justifiable, such as the force of a good example, and the kind of incitement that is obviously illegal, such as the smuggling of arms to rebels or the instigation of sabotage. The drawing of a line of distinction between good and bad may well involve an estimate of motive. What, for example, about the food parcels that were sent to West Berlin, just after the East German risings of June 1953, with an open invitation to East Germans to come and fetch them? I happened to be visiting both sectors of Berlin at about this time, and there was little doubt in anyone's mind but that this was a clever propaganda move on the part of the USA, and not any evidence of real compassion. As a result, many strongly anti-communist East Berlin Christians refused to accept food from these parcels, feeling that it was tainted by bad motives. Others felt that the American people themselves meant well and that if this were a form of cold war, at least food was better than bombs.

The really absurd feature of the whole affair, however, was that every day West Berlin citizens were pouring over into East Berlin to eat in the restaurants there. They did this because of the fantastic rate of exchange. Although salaries and prices were *numerically* not much different in the two parts of Germany, the West German mark was and is worth more than five East German marks, and so would go five times as far in the East as in the West. But East Berliners seldom got oranges or bananas or other kinds of food that needed foreign exchange to buy them.

It seemed to me then, as it does now, that the nations must set themselves the task of finding some monetary system or some other system of exchange that complies with elementary justice. Until this is done I do not see how obviously unjust inequalities, in themselves an incentive to resentment, subversion, and crime, are to be avoided. And by elementary justice I mean that if a man or woman in any part of the world does a good day's work, the standard of living they enjoy should not depend upon the creation of artificial barriers to the exchange of goods, barriers based on power politics. The shilling has the same purchasing power whether it comes from the pocket of a Scottish crofter or that of a Lancashire millworker. If Germany were united, the piece of money representing one hour's work would buy the same amount whether it was earned or spent in East or in West Berlin.

The fact that an artificial barrier across Germany can produce such a difference may be capable of being explained in terms of market prices, but it is nevertheless absurd; and it is wrong, because it produces widespread injustice.

One feature of the cold war that was very marked at the time when I was in Berlin and that still continues, was the steady stream of refugees coming over from East to West Berlin. At that time about 500 a day were passing through the transit camps. A very small trickle was going the other way. One of the present worries of the East German Government is the steady loss of trained scientists and technicians to West Germany. So worrying is it that for some time now they have been allowed to return, if they will, without any fear of punishment. And within East Germany, as in the Soviet Union, scientists and engineers have become a privileged class.

Refugees are not exactly encouraged in general, because they may be a burden and they may contain a percentage of spies or secret agents. But neither are they wholly discouraged, since they often bring with them talent (much talent, in the case of many of the refugees from Nazi Germany to this country and to the USA). More than that, since they are fleeing from a political system that is unpopular in the country to which they come, they are sometimes a useful stick with which to beat a disliked régime. However, it was certainly not made particularly easy for them in Berlin in 1953, where their passport to liberty had to be checked by inquiries in some twenty-nine different offices, in each of which it had to be stamped. It may be easier for the Hungarians now.

The purpose for which I was in Berlin was to attend a small international conference of Friends, called together to discuss, particularly with the help of Friends from East Germany, our experience in relation to the communist-sponsored peace campaigns. One thing that emerged very clearly was that distrust of the genuine character of these peace movements increased with the geographical distance of the participants from actual contact with Soviet citizens.

While I was in China two years later, in 1955, Chinese Christians also asked me what the reaction of British Christians to the work of the World Peace Council was, which they strongly supported. I was obliged to reply, as truthfully as I could, that while many Christians could and did co-operate with the World Peace Council and its national committees, many more agreed with the government view that all communist-sponsored peace campaigns were political rather than moral, probably phoney, and potentially subversive. Leaving aside for the moment the question as to whether this judgement is just, the fact that even a peace campaign can be, or can be regarded as, a form of subversion does illustrate the difficulty of bringing about that complete change of thinking that I believe will be necessary if the world is to be saved from itself. Because some time or other we must get together, even with those whose system of government we dis-like, and talk peace seriously; not as a form of propaganda, but because if we do not, we shall perish together.

The use of armed force as a police method in dealing with *nations* is inevitably being ruled out by the increasingly suicidal nature of the arms themselves. That is an inexorable trend, whether it militates for or against international justice. Yet at the same time the spread of some degree of international morality makes governments wish to appear, in the eyes of the world, to be acting justly. What seems to be absolutely necessary, is that before we reach the stage where any attempt to arraign a 'criminal' nation may mean world suicide, we should attempt to agree on the total elimination of armed force, and the building up of a world opinion which universally rejects and renounces the use of collective and organized violence.

But at the same time we in the richer and more powerful countries must realize that this inevitably means the abandonment of power politics and with it many of the material advantages that we now enjoy.

CHAPTER 11

At present there is very little confidence that total, or even partial, disarmament can come by agreement, in spite of the continuing meetings of the UN Disarmament Commission and its Sub-Committees.

Only once has a formal proposal for total and universal disarmament ever been made in international discussions. In 1927, Litvinov proposed the total abolition of all armed forces on land, sea, and air simultaneously in all States by successive stages over a period of four years. When France objected that such an agreement would give no guarantee of security, Litvinov presented a Draft Convention of 63 Articles which provided for inspection by an international agency and a permanent international control commission to supervise and control the proportional progress of disarmament.

One of the reasons put forward for rejecting the scheme was that if the nations were totally disarmed the colonial peoples would revolt. This might certainly be true to-day. In the context of the modern age this is no excuse for armaments. It is a vital reason for bringing colonialism to an end with the greatest possible speed; and under colonialism I include all enforced government of unwilling peoples, such as those in Eastern Germany or Cyprus. A ballot under UN auspices could be one way of ascertaining whether the people themselves desired self-government and indeed were ready for it. But it must be remembered that self-government, even if inefficient, may be preferred, may even be preferable to an imposed government. That is certainly the principle that is adopted in modern education, where self-discipline is taught by its exercise and no amount of imposed discipline can take its place. The progress of nations such as the Gold Coast (Ghana) and Nigeria has shown what can be done when the will to do it is there. If some of our political leaders had had their way, India would still be an unwilling colony under martial rule instead of being a great force for peace in the modern world, as she is today under the influence of Gandhi and the leadership of Nehru.

There is bound to be strong industrial pressure against the speeding-up of self-determination for the colonies, and they themselves would lose greatly also if self-determination meant the withdrawal of British expert help and financial assistance in connexion with problems of education, building of roads, dams, bridges, and other social needs. But let us not forget those colonies, such as Aden where, in spite of 120 years of British rule, the people are still 79 percent illiterate.[15]

Let us not forget also that Britain is now taking out of the colonies far more than she is giving back. The amount allocated to Colonial Development and Welfare for the year 1955 was £16 million, less than four shillings per annum per person in those territories. Yet even this small amount would be badly missed if it were withdrawn. There are great reserves of friendship for colonial peoples in Britain and self-determination need not and could not mean isolation from all forms of assistance from without. What it would mean is that a British administration would no longer be able to detain prisoners indefinitely without trial, to hang them for the possession of firearms that may in any case have been planted on them by others, or to manacle them with leg irons for periods of up to three months, all of which have been done in Kenya, and all of which methods of 'pacification' go to increase a legacy of hatred and resentment. It may well be true that police methods effective in Britain could not at present keep the peace in Kenya, Singapore, Cyprus, and so on. The question is whether British police, or rather British military forces, should be there at all.

However that may be, and I agree that these questions are arguable, the fact remains that unless the world destroys militarism, scientific weapons will destroy the world. And the main causes of the rot will be selfishness and fear.

15 *Basic Facts and Figures* (U N E S C O), 1954.

Going back to 1927, the then great powers, except for Germany and Turkey, refused even to consider seriously the USSR proposals for total disarmament, so Litvinov subsequently put forward a plan for partial disarmament, and this was discussed in 1929, but never voted on. Then came the great economic slump.

In 1932 the USA proposed the Hoover Plan, which called for a one-third reduction of all armies and the abolition of tanks, large artillery, chemical weapons, and bombing planes: in fact of all modern methods of scientific warfare on land then known. It is interesting to recall the expenditures on armaments (taken as a rounded-off percentage of total Government expenditure) of some of the nations in that year.[16]

Australia	1.2
Canada	2.6
France	26
Germany	13
Italy	24
Japan	35
Norway	15
Sweden	10
Switzerland	16.6
UK	12
USA	18
USSR	6

(Our percentage expenditure on 'defence' in 1955 in the United Kingdom was 32.)

Britain and France consistently opposed any and every suggestion for the limitation and reduction of armaments, and in 1935 the arms race began, in

16 Figures taken from Arthur Guy Enoch's *This War Business*, The Bodley Head, London, 1951. References to sources are given there.

which at first Germany sprang well ahead, and which culminated in World War II. There is a bitter interest in remembering that in 1932 the USA and the USSR were in at least partial agreement on disarmament, but could not get Britain to agree; in recalling also that some of the weapons used against us by Germany in 1939 were actually made in Britain; and in noting that we are again touting for West Germany to buy British armaments.[17]

The atomic bombs changed the situation completely, but they did not change men's habits of thinking and bargaining in terms of power politics and of their own interests. Even although the nations could see the writing on the wall, the plans put forward by the USA (the Baruch plan, which later formed the substance of the Majority Plan), and by the USSR (the Minority Plan) were such as to favour their own security and to leave the other feeling wide open to attack. Neither could have hoped to achieve agreement on such a basis.

It may be worth mentioning here, since we are trying to be realistic and to reach real understanding, the principal reason why the Paris and Stockholm and other peace campaigns of the organization that eventually became the World Peace Council were suspect, not only to the Western governments, but also to those of us who were closely following the course of the discussions on the international control of atomic energy. This was that the proposals that they put forward, and to which they tried to get (and did get) very large numbers of signatures in Western countries, were essentially those of the Minority (the Soviet) Plan.[18] Many of those making the proposals were no doubt entirely honest in believing that they could be a step towards peace. Either of the plans could have been a step towards peace if they had been made in good faith and accepted in good faith. The authors of the Acheson-Lilienthal Report also were entirely sincere in stating that 'the only complete protection for the civilized world from

17 *The Times*, second leader, 5 October 1956.

18 It should in fairness be added that more recent documents of the World Council of Peace have been more objective. In particular the WPC has published a valuable resume of Official Statements pertaining to Disarmament Negotiations between the Great Powers (Vienna, 1956). Its Soviet members, in the Soviet Peace Movement, have also asked the Soviet Government to examine sympathetically the question of legal recognition of war resisters.

the destructive use of scientific knowledge lies in the prevention of war', and they knew that proposals for the international control of atomic energy were only a first step towards this end. The hope was that in solving this one problem, a new pattern of cooperative effort might be established that would be capable of extension to other fields, though not, of course, in the same form. Biological weapons, for instance, could not have been internationally controlled by any comparable means, and conventional weapons were not at first discussed.

Throughout the discussions there have been areas of basic agreement. The agreed goals have been the reduction and regulation of armed forces and of armaments; the elimination of atomic weapons and the use of atomic energy only for peaceful purposes; the setting up of an international system of control and inspection to report violation of agreements. Disagreements have centred on the timing and extent of the various steps, the questions as to which should take place first, and the defining of the functions of the controlling body and of its powers.

Throughout the earlier discussions also, however, there seemed to have been a widespread feeling on both sides that to give way at any point would be a sign of weakness involving loss of prestige. It has even seemed at times as if the discussions themselves, and the bad feelings generated by the imputation of bad motives, have worsened the international situation. At the same time while the dangers of not agreeing have become even more apparent, international events have hardened hearts on either side and proposals have been made and withdrawn until an ordinary citizen who attempts to follow the discussions closely begins to feel really giddy.

Nevertheless there have been major concessions and improvements in mutual understanding. We are learning to be more polite to each other, and that is a help.

Perhaps a very brief resume will show what I mean. In 1946, the Baruch plan called for international control to precede the cessation of atomic bomb manufacture. The Soviet plan wanted destruction of bombs as a first step.

In 1950, the USA, which had previously insisted on separate commissions to discuss the control of nuclear weapons and of conventional armaments, agreed that these two should be merged, and the UN Disarmament Commission was established in January 1952.

During 1952, the USA, Britain, France, and Canada argued that the order of priorities should be: divulging (by stages) and checking of military information under international control; balanced reduction of armed forces (to a ceiling figure of 1 to 1.5 million for the USA, the USSR, and China) and of conventional armaments; prohibition of atomic and other 'weapons of mass; destruction'.

The USSR wanted the order reversed and in particular proposed the reduction of all armed forces by one-third within one year. (The propaganda of the World Peace Council echoed this proposal.) In 1955 the USSR accepted the proposals, repeated in the meantime by Britain and France, that armed forces should be reduced to a ceiling of 1 to 1½ million for the Big Three (the USA, USSR, and China) and to 650,000 for Britain and France, but asked also that 'as one of the first measures for the execution of the programme for the reduction of armaments and the prohibition of atomic weapons, States possessing atomic and hydrogen weapons shall undertake to discontinue tests of these weapons', and that 'States possessing military, naval and air bases in the territories of other States shall undertake to liquidate such bases'.

They also proposed that during the first stage of reduction of armaments and prohibition of atomic weapons, the UN International Control Organ should have 'control posts at large ports, at railway junctions, on main motor highways and in aerodromes' to prevent surprise attacks, and that during the second stage there should be added 'inspection on a continuing basis'.

They accepted the Anglo-French proposals that 75 per cent of the reduction of armed forces and conventional weapons should take place *before* the prohibition and elimination of atomic, hydrogen, and other weapons of mass destruction should come into force.

The proposal for the liquidation of military bases on foreign soil was not, of course, acceptable to the USA, nor were the suggestions relating to international control regarded as adequate. At the Summit meeting of 18 July 1955, President Eisenhower offered his 'open skies' plan for an exchange of military blueprints and aerial reconnaissance between the USA and the USSR, as the best warning against danger of a sudden attack by either on the other.

President Bulganin, in a reasonable and courteous letter of 19 September 1955, pointed out to President Eisenhower that 'Under present international conditions both our countries are not acting singly'. US forces, as he said, are stationed in England, West Germany, Italy, France, Spain, North Africa, Greece, Turkey, and other countries of the Near and Middle East, in Japan, in Taiwan, and in the Philippines. There are also armed forces of other States under US command. While at the same time 'the Soviet Union on its side has united militarily with several allied States'.

If it were only the USA and the USSR that had aerial reconnaissance, all these other armed forces and military installations would be left out of account, but would they in any case agree to be included, President Bulganin asked?

And if they were, would that really help, unless armaments were also reduced, and atomic weapons prohibited?

At this time President Eisenhower was ill, and he then only replied briefly to say that he did not regard his plan 'as a cure-all', but as a means of creating 'a fresh atmosphere which would dispel much of the present fear and suspicion'.

Essentially the USA has concentrated attention on the need, before all else, of a comprehensive air-ground inspection scheme. To the great disappointment of many people, the original suggestion of 28 May 1952 of a ceiling of 1 to 1½ million was withdrawn by the USA, and on 3 April 1956, they made a proposal of a ceiling of 2½ million for the USA, the USSR, and China, and of 750,000 for Britain and France. Since the Soviet forces and those of China are at present estimated to be about 4 million each, while those of the USA are about 2,900,000 and of Britain 800,000, this would mean a manpower reduction of over 37 per cent for the communist powers as compared with less than 14 per cent for the USA and about 6 per cent for Britain.

The Soviet reaction to this was to announce a unilateral reduction of their military manpower by 1,200,000 and later (on 12 July 1956) to accept the new ceiling levels of 2½ million, etc., combining this with a sharp attack on the Western military alliances, NATO, SEATO, and the Baghdad Pact. They protested against the suggestion that disarmament must wait for political settlements. They have since accepted the idea of limited aerial reconnaissance, and at the time of writing, the USA seems to be on the point of making fresh proposals.

Mr Dulles has said recently that 'Political settlements help disarmament and disarmament helps political settlements. . . . A settlement on Germany would not be practical without at least a partial settlement of the disarmament problem.'

The fact that past production of nuclear weapons cannot be checked is now accepted, and has helped to relegate the elimination of such weapons to the last stage of any disarmament proposals. If this means, however, as apparently it does, that until all major political problems are settled the nations possessing nuclear weapons intend to hold on to them and to sufficient military organization to be able to use them 'as a last resort', then there is little hope that they will ever be really eliminated from political calculations.

It seems to me utterly unrealistic to suppose that even if our present political problems: the division of Germany and of Korea, the rivalries between the USA and the USSR, the military and economic hold that these two great Powers have on the various European countries, the rising nationalism of the Arab States, the existence of Israel, the demand for self-determination in the Colonies, the two Chinas – to mention only some; it seems quite unrealistic to suppose that if these problems were settled, other urgent political problems would not arise. The very changes of which I have written previously – the uneven changes of population, the growing industrialization or mechanization of countries which, technically speaking, are now undeveloped, the possibilities of scientific inventions involving raw materials in short supply or of uneven distribution which may upset the balance of power, the resentment of the Asian-African peoples at their treatment as inferiors, as well as others I have not discussed at all – are bound to bring new problems to be solved, and new conflicts to settle.

To suppose that these will be solved peacefully in a world that has not learned to look on war – not conflict but war – as a crime, is a hallucination.

If it is then argued that crimes are committed and must be punished, I can only repeat that we cannot afford to retain war as a punishment for the crime of war, in a world where scientific weapons of mass destruction will soon be a possibility for any nation having nuclear power stations. I see no escape whatever from the inexorable logic of this argument. I can only suggest that we who call ourselves civilized should lead the way by making our children regard war as one of those crimes which, like cannibalism, are so horrible that no civilized person, certainly no civilized *nation,* would commit it. This argument applies as much to civil war and to 'police actions' as to international war, for it is the whole idea of settling group differences or any other problem by means of armed violence that must be eradicated.

The inquiry with which this book began set on one side arguments based essentially on the religious principles fundamental to the Christian faith as Friends understand them. Yet again and again it seems to me that the inexorable trend of scientific and historical facts and the teachings of Christian morality lead in the same direction. 'For the wages of sin is death' is as true now as when it was written, it is as true of the world as of any single human being.

CHAPTER 12

Whatever we do as individuals or as a nation, there are risks that we must take. Sometimes, if the danger is immediate, we take a risk without even thinking about it, as when a man who cannot swim plunges into a river to save a child. It may be too deep for him also; he hardly stops to consider that fact. More often we take calculated risks. This applies as much to the Christian as to the atheist, to the politician as to the pacifist. It is generally taken for granted that the Christian, and especially the Christian pacifist, takes risks involving his faith; the politician and the materialist, risks based on reasoning.

If the Christian pacifist like myself is wrong, if God is not a God of love, if goodness is not the most powerful force in the world, then not only may this civilization perish, but evil may in the long run prevail. If we are right, then this civilization may perish all the same, but goodness will not perish with it; and whatever the immediate and apparent consequences, it is imperative that men and nations shall not use evil means to achieve apparently good ends. And evil means we define as those actions that are contrary to the law of love: Whatsoever things ye would that men should do to you, do ye even so to them; those things the doing of which debases the man who does them.

This way of thinking and acting, however, is by no means necessarily opposed to the way of reason. On the contrary, the Christian pacifist would insist that it is the soundest form of reason, because it moves with the stream of God's purpose and not against it. The politician or atheist or humanist who is not a pacifist by conviction based on Christian ethics may well come to the same conclusions, if he considers honestly and sincerely the long-term lessons of history and follows the dictates of his conscience. It is not arrogance but faith on the part of the Christian pacifist that impels him to say that *true* reason and an *enlightened* conscience must move men in the same way.

I hope I shall not be accused of special pleading if I take as an example the case of military conscription. The fact that military conscription is essentially a training of young men to kill their fellowmen is simply not faced by a great many kind-hearted people. They think of it in terms of an extension of physical education, in terms of development of character, of social mixing, of learning a trade and seeing the world, of fair sharing of a social responsibility, of learning discipline. When conscription was extended into peacetime there were a great many responsible and educated women who clamoured for its extension to young women also, on these grounds.

It is true that in any future nuclear war conscripts will not meet and kill an enemy face to face, as they do in jungle warfare. They will read charts, make calculations, pull levers and press buttons, to rain down death and torture on millions of men, women, and children whom they have never seen, in retaliation perhaps for the death and torture that has come to those in their own country, or in anticipation of it. The training to kill is basic, whatever other training accompanies it.

But it is reported that in the recent debate on National Service not one speaker in the House of Commons put forward the arguments often used before, that military conscription is a good thing in itself. That argument is no longer a reasonable one. Far from being a useful extension of education, its effect is such that young conscripts may often be seen in trains, either reading 'comics' or just sitting for hours on end, doing nothing. Meanwhile industry is handicapped by lack of young trainees, apprentices, and technicians. Many conscripts do receive some useful training, but others feel that it was a sheer waste of time and that they learned nothing except ways of avoiding hard work.

Both sides of the House were agreed in principle that conscription should be abolished. The question of timing of its abolition was debated on the grounds of national security only. Its continuance is urged because it is alleged that we cannot do without it unless we abandon our present foreign policy and the military commitments that go with it. And yet many of those who support, or do not actively oppose conscription believe our present foreign policy to be mistaken. One of the indictments of compulsory military training, here as elsewhere, is that it permits and encourages a belligerent foreign policy. Nor is the training of young men to do as they are ordered likely to produce intelligent citizens capable of informed and constructive criticism of foolish, obstinate, or panicky political policies. It is much more likely to produce men who think first in terms of force: just the kind of thinking that we must learn to avoid in an atom-conscious world with major problems to solve in respect of population and racial adjustments. There is grave danger to mankind to-day, and in the future, in the fact that here and in France, in the USA and the USSR, and in many other countries, we are training young men at a most impressionable age to blind obedience to orders from leaders, from the State, from anyone with a loud voice and an appearance of authority. In this new age of atoms and automation we need, not mechanized robots, but men who can think for themselves, who can see through false propaganda, who have initiative and self-discipline, who are responsible citizens, neither overawed by bureaucracy nor sick of the very idea of 'service'.

All these, whether one agrees with them or not, are reasonable arguments. The objection to military conscription on spiritual grounds goes much farther than this. It is, of course, part of an objection to war as such, but it goes much farther than that also. The young men who are now registering were infants or were not born when conscription was introduced into this country in 1939. They have had little or no chance of forming a personal opinion on the moral issues involved, for they have grown up in a community that has accepted conscription. The Christian Church, apart from a few small groups, has silently or actively acquiesced in it. These young people are being conditioned to believe that two years' training to kill, torture, and destroy is an inevitable if regrettable part of citizenship and even of Christian citizenship. This in itself is a violation of the sacredness of their reason and of their personality. It inculcates wrong values and trains them in habits of violence. Conscription removes them from the influence of home and friends and exposes them to moral dangers which many of them are not yet self-disciplined enough to resist. It teaches them a response and an attitude to evil and to aggression which is the exact opposite of the teaching of Christ. It encourages a double morality, in that it trains them to believe that a man under orders, or a community in general, may commit crimes that a private individual may not do, and would shudder to do.

It is, of its kind, just the sort of conditioning that we most criticize and fear when the communists do it to their own young people. We have, indeed, so conditioned ourselves that we allow Army and RAF officers to go into our schools in order to tell small boys what fine careers and what splendid technical training the fighting forces can offer. What is equally certain is that any good aspects of training could and should be attained in other ways, in technical schools and colleges, in school camps, by scouts, by youth clubs, by an extra year at school, by organized foreign travel, by international work camps, by opportunities for technical training and service abroad, without the military training and operations that now contaminate the phrase 'National Service'.

Both reason and morality point to the conclusion that compulsory military training should come to an end.

In discussing the calculated risks involved in the continuance of our present policy of military preparedness in general, I shall try to do so as objectively as possible, without assuming the basic religious tenets of the Christian faith as I understand it. People differ more widely on questions of morality than scientists differ on questions of fact. Perhaps it would be true to say that while most people would agree that morality should guide our actions, some see morality in terms of the kind of personal behaviour that fits in with their conception of God – the ultimate reality; others see it in terms of its probable effect, its practicability, or its relation to the authoritative pronouncements of the Church or *The Times*.

The orthodox conception of the just war is based on the latter idea of morality. A war is said to be just if the injuries to be anticipated from the war do not outweigh the injustices which it is intended to rectify or prevent;

if peaceful means for accomplishing the same end are neither available nor adequate and in the proper political authority, after considering these questions and moved only by the desire to promote justice, has sanctioned the war.

What then are the best and the worst that we can expect from (1) our present course of action as a nation and as a community of nations, (2) partial or total unilateral disarmament, (3) partial or total universal disarmament?

It may be that the possession of nuclear weapons will stave off war between the Powers that now have them, that in time the habit of having to find peaceful solutions to our mutual problems will teach us to live together, that we shall gradually make the United Nations more inclusive and objective and have more respect for its decisions, that we shall find some way of agreeing on a form of international control that will make us feel comparatively secure, and that by the exercise of a similar control we shall be able to prevent the development of these or other scientific weapons by other nations as long as peace lasts. In the meantime we shall be steadily setting on one side for military purposes a large proportion of our scientific and technical manpower and a very considerable percentage of our financial resources. We shall continue to train young men and women, as conscripts or as volunteers, in the ways of war. We shall teach them that although world war is unthinkable, we may find it expedient to risk limited wars in order to protect our British interests, or in order to pacify unruly natives, and in these limited wars they will use whatever ghastly weapons we suppose to be necessary for victory or for the discipline of those who are so wicked as to oppose us. They will learn to do as a duty what would be a crime in civil life, and having done it they will return to civil life and to the bearing of children who will learn the same things. That is about the best that can be hoped for from our present course of action.

This also assumes that all the problems and conflicts that will arise in the future can be dealt with by an extension of the methods that we have used in the past.

I find it difficult to believe that this is so, or that if we do go on thinking and acting in the same way as now, we shall for long avoid the dreadful catastrophe which is the other side of the coin, the risk that is deliberately being taken. I do not believe it to be inconceivable that our civilization is doomed. Other civilizations have perished: other species have disappeared because they could not adapt themselves to new circumstances or a new environment. We no longer have the mammoth or the sabre-toothed tiger. The risk is not even so much that our civilization should disappear, but that it should disappear so horribly, and so needlessly.

Before considering whether the elimination of war through total and universal disarmament is humanly speaking possible, I want to try to consider what the risks of such a policy would be. First of all we should take the case of unilateral disarmament, and even here we must consider separately the possible effects of partial and of total disarmament. What are the best and the worst to be anticipated from either? Are they better or worse than the effects of our present policies?

Unilateral *partial* disarmament by Britain might bring her armaments down to the level of those of other small countries which are also industrialized but which are neither so heavily dependent upon the USA nor upon distant and, at times, troublesome colonies. Any major disarmament would have to be preceded by withdrawal from or modification of our commitments under various military pacts. The effect might be to stimulate the discussion of international disarmament on a more urgent and effective basis; it would release funds for social and educational work for industrial improvements, for tax relief, and for participation in schemes of international technical aid. One suggestion made at Geneva in July 1955 by M. Edgar Faure was that the money and materials made available by limitation of armaments should 'be applied to the tasks of aiding and equipping under-developed territories and under-privileged peoples'.

The risks are obvious. It is not very likely, as has sometime been suggested, that the USA or the USSR would actually and immediately occupy Britain, if Britain withdrew from her military commitments, but there would almost certainly be the stronger economic and political pressure for the American bases to remain and to be reinforced. Britain would still be vulnerable in case of war and would no longer be able to exert military pressure on and offer military defence to other nations. It is possible, for example that South Africa might forcibly assume control of the High Commission Territories, Bechuanaland, Swaziland, and Basutoland. Our own record in these countries is nothing to be very proud of, but they would not willingly become part of the Union of South Africa. Our standards of living might suffer if our colonies seceded or were annexed, or if our lines of communication were blocked. The process of demobilization might cause a serious unemployment problem. Britain might well lose her place on the Security Council and much of her influence in UN affairs. Her level would be that of, say, one of the Scandinavian powers.

Even unilateral *total* disarmament on the part of Britain, or any other single country, would not prevent a nuclear war. Total disarmament would mean the complete disbanding of all military organization and the complete withdrawal from all military commitments. It would necessarily involve a refusal voluntarily to permit military bases to remain on British soil. It would have to be accompanied by a declaration of neutrality and an offer to permit any kind of inspection within our own country. It would mean the withdrawal of spies and secret agents from other countries, and the maintenance only of genuine civilian police in countries under our control. At the best it could mean that we might set an example to other nations, that we would break the vicious spiral of rivalry – armaments – war – new rivalries – more deadly armaments – more suicidal war. It would give us the opportunity of really helping many here and in other countries who now suffer and die from preventable disease, hunger, or other forms of need. There are a million people blind from preventable disease in the British Commonwealth alone. I thought of them when I saw a recent poster showing a Civil Defence official bandaging the eyes of a hypothetical casualty in a future nuclear war. His uniform alone would save the sight of some of these poor blind people right now.

We would be forced to negotiate in a spirit of mutual seeking or mutual advantage. It would give us a very real incentive to improve techniques of negotiation and conciliation in disputes between other nations. We would try to promote respect for the World Court of Justice.

The case against unilateral disarmament, partial or total, rests mainly on the assumption that if we were militarily vulnerable we could at once be invaded and used as a base in any future war, as Norway was in World War II. That if we were invaded by the USSR our democratic form of government would be suppressed, our children would be taught to be atheists, and that they would be conscripted to fight on the communist side. The destruction of civilization altogether, it is suggested, would be better than a world in which Christian ideals had disappeared and evil was master.

There is a strong argument against unilateral total disarmament on the ground that it would be almost superhumanly difficult to bring it about, but the argument that if it had been brought about it could result in the disappearance of Christian ideals is one that both reason and faith reject. If total disarmament were undertaken only on the ground that it would make a nation safe, that it would be an insurance against attack, that would be a powerful argument but probably an untrustworthy one. The revulsion of public feeling if and when an attack came might have a disastrous effect. But if in fact a nation decided to disarm because it was believed to be the right thing to do, then that nation would be spiritually strong enough to stand up to any attack on its faith. Its children would be grounded in Christian principles and would have been taught how to face spiritual evil and to oppose it, peacefully. 'Fear not them which kill the body, but are not able to kill the soul' would be basic to all education. Is this a perfectionist hope? The spirits of the martyrs say 'No'.

And are we anyhow, as individuals, all that much superior to the Russians or the Chinese, now? The suggestion that we, in the West, who actually used atomic bombs and who first invented the rigged hydrogen bomb, have a monopoly of all the Christian virtues, just strikes me as simply fantastic.

CHAPTER 13

Much of what I have said in previous chapters has been based on evidence concerning the terrible effects of nuclear weapons and the certainty that if and when all nations are capable of making and testing them, or even before that time, the world itself will be in dreadful peril, with or without actual war. It has been argued that, even if those who believe in hydrogen bombs as a means of keeping the peace are right, it is still essential that the nations shall, separately and together, urgently seek ways and means of totally abandoning the use of force and war preparations, even for 'police' purposes, and that this research is an immediate imperative, not a distant aim.

Is the fear of consequences an unworthy motive? It is not the best motive for seeking to act uprightly, but it is the point from which an erring world may have to begin. 'Except ye repent, ye shall all likewise perish' is the first lesson to be learnt from Hiroshima and Nagasaki. It is not enough to regret that certain consequences may occur. We have sinned: and the consequences are those of our sin. Until at least some of us realize and admit this I do not see how we can go on to the next step, which is to change our ways of thinking and acting, and the ways in which we train our children to think and act.

The attempt that has been made so far to obtain agreement on partial disarmament has not involved any radical changes in our ways of thinking at all. We still think in terms of national advantage and of power politics. We still want to get our own way, to get the better of other people. This game can be played without nuclear or other weapons of mass destruction, but it is liable to lead to war; and once war has begun on a large enough scale, any kind of weapon can be made and used. Partial disarmament, even if universal, would not alter this state of affairs.

Suppose there is eventual acceptance by the USSR, the USA, and other UN powers of complete ground inspection, and of a reduction of their armies to agreed ceilings. This would imply also a willingness to lay wide open all laboratories in which research of any kind is being conducted, secret research especially but not exclusively, and it would involve the employment of a large body of scientific and technical inspectors. These would have to be really expert in every field, for they must not only understand what is being done, but what the outcome of the work might be. The difficulty of detecting weapons of chemical and biological warfare was once illustrated by saying that they might be made in any brewery. If this led to the abolition of breweries some of us would not mind.

All this could perhaps be done, but there are no signs whatever at present that even the most elementary and preliminary steps involved are being undertaken. No inquiries have been made, for example, of professional scientific bodies as to whether many of their numbers would be willing to be trained for such work. Or if they have, the inquiries have not come through to any of the scientific committees or councils of which I have knowledge. The omission of any consideration of this question makes me doubt seriously whether even our present disarmament proposals are honest ones. But let us assume that they are honest. Where would we go from there?

The present, still very hypothetical plans for partial disarmament envisage that at a later stage, the nations which have nuclear weapons, having first undertaken not to use them except in retaliation, would destroy their stocks. They would retain the fissionable material in them for use in nuclear power stations and for other peaceful purposes only. Continuing air-ground inspection would ensure that violations did not occur. If they did, it is understood that the alert having been given in good time, all nations would combine against the delinquent nation. If all went smoothly and there were no violations, the ground would be cleared for a further agreement. This would involve eventual disarmament to the levels regarded as essential for internal security, plus those which would be contributed to a common pool, under the UN or some other form of world organization. These would have to be sufficient to prevent armed attack by one nation upon another. Possibly the UN forces would retain the monopoly of nuclear weapons of all kinds.

The apparent advantage of this gradual method is that it seems to involve only administrative and technical detail; it does not imply a change of heart on the part of any very large number of people. Reductions could be brought about without any major change of political thinking. If carefully planned, demobilization need cause no unemployment and reorientation of armament factories need cause no dislocation of industry. The eventual effect would undoubtedly be an improvement in the economic situation of all the countries concerned, and the conservation of world resources for genuine world needs. This in itself would be an encouragement to continue disarmament, perhaps even to the point where constant control and inspection by internationally employed and scientifically trained men and women could be dispensed with. We do not now have to search private homes continuously for hidden arms, although in a time of civil strife this may be necessary.

I do not say that this gradual method is hopeless or that if honestly undertaken it could not be successful. What does seem hopeless to me is that it should be attempted *concurrently* with a continuance of power politics; with the deliberate encouragement to rearm of Germany and Japan; with the reluctance on the part of the great Powers even to discontinue nuclear tests and call an armaments truce; and, most of all, with the continuance of military training and thinking both in schools, through the Services and in general through all the media of propaganda. This is not sense. And not one of the great Powers has any monopoly of this nonsense.

When, for example, one reads of the 'sermonettes' issued by the White House with a high moral tone of disapproval of the Russians for continuing with nuclear tests,[19] when the Americans were themselves carrying out such tests constantly, any kind of self-righteous hypocrisy seems possible.

But in spite of a professed longing for peace, the Soviet government is still giving military training to millions of young men and women and indeed to

19 *The Times*, 10 September 1956.

schoolchildren, and is teaching them to think of a war of defence as something noble. Their former ideal of total disarmament has never been revived. It is impossible not to believe that this is because they realize, as we should also realize for ourselves, that disarmament and Empire are incompatible, although disarmament and Commonwealth are not. The Soviet government for long refused to admit that any of her Eastern European 'allies' were unwilling allies. Disarmament would be the final test of that for all of them, as for our own colonies also.

I think it may be relevant here to point out that it would be far less difficult to control universal *total* disarmament than universal *partial* disarmament. Armaments of any kind require military organization and military establishments. It is generally accepted now that inspection could not check past production of fissionable material, the stockpiling of which is steadily increasing. Nor could control and inspection operate over a continuing arms race. It would be effective only as a means of checking every step of an agreed disarmament programme of immense detail. The task of the inspectorate appointed to control *partial* disarmament would be not only to spot new research activities that might lead to weapons hitherto unknown, but to report on the level of activities that were permitted up to a certain point, but not beyond that point. There would be a continuous atmosphere of suspicion, for war itself would not have been eliminated from national thinking and war itself involves deceit and rivalry and distrust.

Total disarmament would not be an extreme form of partial disarmament; however, it would be something quite different, and its form of control and inspection would be quite different. At present our attitude is 'If you eat my grandmother, I'll eat yours. But if you will agree not to eat my grandmother, I'll agree not to eat yours either, but I will jolly well look out to see that you are not beginning to boil the water in the saucepan.' What we need to do is to develop a horror of cannibalism, a horror of the crime of war.

Total disarmament means not only the abolition of military organization, of armament factories, of armies, of the naval and air forces, but the re-education of men and women everywhere to abhor the very idea of war.

Assuming for the time being that this could be done, it would mean that every man or woman would be an inspector to ensure that no form of military organization, no secret military research, no stockpiling or manufacture of armaments remained or was renewed in their *own* country. Where there is no military organization there need be no secrecy. If there were no secrecy, military organization could not be hidden. If disarmament were total, *any* military organization or research would be illegal and could be treated as such within the nation itself. 'Nothing' is a much more absolute level than any other. For a time, perhaps, the employment of scientists and engineers of all nationalities would, as I suggested earlier, give additional security in nuclear power stations, where only a few very knowledgeable people could know what was actually going on, but without military organization even armaments themselves would be useless, and so would spies.

The really important thing is that men and women themselves should learn to abhor war and all preparations for war, not only in one country – although some country must set an example – but in every country. And that they should learn to abhor it so much that they were willing to accept the read-justments that the absence of war and of the sanction of force might mean. It would be absolutely necessary to be clear on that point in any large-scale effort at adult education. The education of children for a world without war could be simple. They would fight each other still, no doubt. When a can-nibal is reformed, he does not then scruple to cut the head off a cauliflower. But between the rough-and-tumble of children and the horrors of scientific warfare there is a difference not of degree but of kind: a difference as big as between a tiny rivulet and the fathomless ocean. And all warfare in the industrialized world of the future will be scientific warfare, even though for the time being, and until technical knowledge is more widely spread, some limited forms of war may be possible. The quarrels of children or of adults may be the roots of behaviour that could develop into communal belliger-ency. But there are other forms of childish behaviour that are recognized as antisocial. These are socially discouraged and not accepted as a basic principle of national behaviour, however natural in some children.

The really vicious thing about the present acceptance of war preparations and of conscription as a necessary part of national life is that it gives a veneer of patriotic respectability to those attitudes and impulses that are, in fact, anti-social. At present every form of propagandist medium is capable of being used, and often is used, to accentuate our differences with other nations and to whip up patriotic emotions. Personal abuse of those who oppose us takes the place of reasoned and restrained discussion. Their weaknesses are exposed, instead of our considering whether our own behaviour has contributed to the situation and whether we could do anything to remedy it.

Children naturally love adventure and pageantry. The mechanism of military advertisement is perfected to make the most of this appeal. No national procession or display seems complete without the participation of military forces, often in gaily-coloured uniforms, riding wonderful horses, or playing stirring music. We have almost abandoned the old-style non-military carnival, more's the pity.

The boys in many of our public schools are brought up to consider a military career as an honourable profession. The fact that war involves many admirable qualities, such as courage, endurance, self-sacrifice, intelligence, and skill, lends support to this supposition. So do the ideas commonly held, that war protects the weak, upholds justice, and is the guardian of ideals. Nevertheless it is not true. War no longer protects the weak, if ever it did. The strong and the weak suffer alike in modern war. But war preparations strike hard at the weak all over the world. Men, women, and children suffer in their millions to-day, because the money and effort that might have been spent in helping them is used instead on military organization, military display, military research, military supplies and military training, in all the wealthier nations.

War does not uphold justice. Justice would require a much more equitable distribution of the world's resources. What the powerful nations understand by justice is the very reverse of this. They mean the protection of their own interests, the enforcement of treaties made to their own advantage. If this were recognized for the kind of selfishness that it is, it would no longer be possible for war and war service to be regarded as honourable. Men and women *are* capable of courage and self-sacrifice, and these could be better employed in the relief of suffering than in the protection of British interests. Men and women *can* endure great hardship and danger, they can accept a lowering of their standards of living, they can be offered 'blood, toil, tears, and sweat' and take them, in the interests of war, but it is always supposed that they could not do this in the interests of peace. Why not? Is it because peace offers so little emotional stimulus, and need this be so?

It is easy to persuade a nation that it is fighting for justice or for the preservation of ideals, because they see the warlike activities of the enemy for the vileness that they are, and do not recognize that their actions are likewise vile. War can never protect ideals, it destroys them. Ideals cannot be put into cold storage and taken out again when they are needed. They decay. Morality deteriorates with neglect, so that what is regarded as revolting at the beginning of a war becomes justified as necessary for victory as the war goes on. War means death, torture, lingering suffering, loss of homes, loss of loved ones, all for thousands or even millions of quite innocent people. Is this the way to promote justice or preserve ideals? Of course it is not.

I believe that real security can only be found, if at all, in a world without the injustices that now exist, and without arms. If, instead of a vain search for a partial disarmament formula that would give absolute security all round (still less for a formula that would give each side more security than the other) the Great Powers were to get together and quite frankly admit that this search is vain, we might get somewhere. We should at least be talking sense, and that would be the beginning of a clearing of suspicion and of a mutual facing of the real problems, the elimination of injustice on the one hand and of military organization on the other.

CHAPTER 14

The Atlantic Charter, framed in 1941 by Winston Churchill and Franklin D. Roosevelt, formed the starting point of a series of pronouncements that finally took shape in the Charter of the United Nations. It contained these words:

> All nations of the world, for realistic as well as spiritual reasons, must come to the abandonment of the use of force.

That was more than fifteen years ago, before the USA entered the war, and four years before the first atomic bomb. If it were realistic then, how much more realistic should it be now to abandon the use of force. I do not believe that this would be impossible. I think that there are problems ahead of us so great that drastic changes in our ways of thinking and acting are absolutely necessary to deal with them. There are two ways in which such changes might come. One is the way of the compulsion of experience, the whip and spur of historical inevitability, the coercion of facts. That is the hard and bitter way. The other is the way of foresight, of preparation, of imagination. It is also the way of moral compulsion. It may be no less hard, but it is not bitter.

But most people are not able to make the effort of imagination that is necessary. They are too accustomed to being led. They can rise to great heights of courage and sacrifice, but not usually without leadership. Two kinds of such leadership exist. The first is leadership from above. The other is leadership from within. Very often the second does have to precede the first. Those people who see clearly the necessity of changed thinking must themselves undertake the discipline of thinking in new ways and must persuade others to do so. If personal pacifism is ever to become national and international pacifism, those who see clearly what is involved must be faithful to their convictions and to their reason, no matter how politically ineffective and wasted their personal effort may seem at the time of making it.

When John Woolman saw clearly that it was wrong for one man to enslave another and for human beings to be bought and sold, he first decided that he himself could no longer make out such Bills of Sale. Then he personally refused to benefit by the services of slaves, gently explaining his attitude to their masters, his friends, as he insisted on paying for his entertainment in their homes, or refused to eat sugar grown by slave labour. He made it his task to persuade his fellow-members of the Society of Friends to renounce the holding of slaves, which they eventually did as a body. And meanwhile others were tackling the difficult problems of educating the Church on the one hand and Parliament on the other, not forgetting that true justice might involve compensation to slaveholders.

It has been rightly pointed out that Britain gave up slavery just in time: before the industrial revolution. If slaves had become machine-minders, the abolition of slavery and of the slave-trade would have become more difficult by an order of magnitude. The fact that some other nations have not yet eliminated slavery did not prevent Britain from doing so once the wrongness of slavery had become apparent. We can engage in unilateral action even to our own disadvantage when our national conscience is touched. I believe that we could take unilateral action, if need be, in respect of military organization also, if we realized not only the utter folly of our present way of action, but the absolute necessity that we who claim to be politically mature should set an example, realizing clearly what the economic consequences would be and what the immediate risks might be.

The fact that it took a civil war to free the slaves in America has sometimes been curiously put forward, by members of the Tribunals before which conscientious objectors come, as a justification for war. Whatever may have been the causes of that conflict, the bitterness that still remains in the South is rather evidence that that way of settling differences was not only wrong but stupid, and that the building up of public opinion to reject both force and selfishness is an absolute imperative for lasting goodwill.

I mentioned before that in order to do this it would be necessary and would not be difficult to teach children the ways of peace. Statesmen who have failed to agree on disarmament might turn their attention to this. It would be an easier task. It is sometimes suggested that nations should appoint Ministries of Peace to replace their Ministries of War. The reply is given that the Foreign Office is essentially a Ministry of Peace. But its record does not bear this out. Certainly we have no record of officials being sent by the Foreign Office into schools to teach the children that war has become an anachronism, a relic of a savage past, and that peace can and should provide the sacrifices and the adventure that war has offered. Instead, we still have Cadet Corps, Officers' Training Corps, Boys' Battalions, and other incentives to children to stick their heads in the sand and ignore the lessons of the past fifty years.

I believe that failing any guidance from the Church or from statesmen, teachers could and should consider this problem with the greatest seriousness and urgency themselves. The education that children receive is constantly undergoing change. It is modified to correspond to the world in which they have to live. This is particularly so in those countries, such as Russia, where a realization of the need for technical advance has given a strong scientific and technical bias to the primary and secondary stages of education. In China also, the need to improve sanitation and to eliminate corruption has led to a most astounding and spectacular success in large-scale education, even of adults, on these two matters. Whatever else may be found to criticize in the present China scene or in the ways in which it has been achieved, recent travellers to China have nothing but praise for the way in which flies and other noxious insects have been eliminated on the one hand, and honesty in trade and the abolition of bribery and graft have been both encouraged and achieved on the other.

What can be done in one field can be done in another, by means which are in keeping with our own democratic traditions. Parent-teacher associations should discuss the educational needs of a world in which war must be unthinkable. If, as I believe, reason and conscience combine to demand such a change, it does in fact only need a little initiative, perhaps a little courage, to suggest such discussions even in the most conservative of staff common rooms. I question very much whether any enthusiasm for the retention of military training in schools would be found among the majority of parents. There might be hesitation on the ground that other nations would not follow our example if our educational system were deliberately geared to a warless world. If we wait for others to set us an example we ought to be ashamed of ourselves, and if we wait for simultaneous agreement we may wait forever.

Children, even though they sometimes fight, are also very willing to be friendly. They do not suspect each other of double-dealing. They neither understand nor care about national boundaries and have no race prejudice until this has taught them by example.

> *You've got to be taught, before it's too late,*
> *Before you are six, or seven, or eight,*
> *To hate all the people your relatives hate.*
> *You've got to be carefully taught.*[20]

They are willing to learn, and the ways of peace and cooperation fit in more naturally with the behaviour we expect of them as individuals, than the ways of war and of national selfishness. If they are selfish, we try to teach them to share their toys. We encourage a team spirit. We teach them that it is right to tell the truth, wrong to tell lies; right to be kind, wrong to be cruel.

We do this not necessarily because we believe in certain doctrines concerning the existence and nature of God, nor even because we consciously apply certain ethical principles, but because life is more reliable, more congenial, if people co-operate with one another, if a man's word can be trusted and if

20 From the song 'You've got to be carefully taught' from *South Pacific*, by Richard Rogers and Oscar Hammerstein.

cruelty is minimized. When I say 'we', I do mean here the majority of normal fathers and mothers. The fact that some parents teach their children to steal does not make us do so. In some countries or in some circumstances standards differ: courtesy or hospitality may be regarded by some people as more important than absolute truth-speaking, for example. This does not make us modify our own values to correspond, once we have decided what kind of education we prefer our own children to have.

But whatever our values or our standards, children do absorb them pretty readily, and what is taught in childhood sticks hard. The British and Americans found that out in Germany, when having taught the post-war generation that militarism was wrong and foolish, they later encouraged Dr Adenauer to reintroduce the idea of military conscription. In place after place, the young people themselves reacted strongly against it; though not always in a disciplined or non-violent way, because their initial training had been superimposed on a period of military occupation and of upheaval.

The new world needs much more than co-existence. It needs ways of living together peacefully and co-operatively, and these ways young people educated in the principles of peace could help to find. There is no need to eliminate adventure, pageantry, and friendly competition from life. Children need adventure so much that they are willing to risk security for it, and wise parents let them. In the world of the future, with newly discovered scientific and technical methods making their impact on ancient and primitive cultures, there will be plenty of room for dangerous and breathtaking adventure, plenty of room for courageous experiment.

Any government that was really determined to replace techniques of war by techniques of peaceful change could find plenty of work for young people willing and anxious to help, training and travel being part of the job in very many cases. The way has been partly blazed already. There are the UN Observers appointed by the Peace Observation Commission established by the UN in 1950. This Commission was given the task of observing and reporting on 'the situation in any area where there exists international tension, the continuance of which is likely to endanger the maintenance of international peace and security'. Its Observers have done valuable work. They have reduced the danger of frontier incidents merely by being there; and where fighting has occurred they have been able to assess primary responsibility on the spot. It would have been better had there been enough of them to form a neutral belt along contested frontiers. Such Observer units would find a valuable place in any scheme of disarmament, and they could and should be unarmed themselves, even if it sometimes meant danger. They can, of course, only function with the consent of the Government in whose country they are stationed; and they are not police.

The UN Force sent to Egypt, with the consent of the Egyptian government, is an intermediate stage between a UN Army and a genuine police force with international personnel. A UN Army would be unnecessary in an unarmed world, and useless or dangerous in one armed with nuclear weapons, or capable of making them. A police force with international training and personnel would have the advantage that it could less easily be used for repressive measures.

There are many young people who now spend their holidays or more extended periods at international work camps, voluntarily doing useful jobs together with young men and women of other countries, living simply, talking hard, and laughing together as well. Some of them save up the fare to travel by the cheapest routes, some are helped by international organizations, others earn their way. There are organizations of people right now who are willing to give lodging for a night or two to any traveller in the cause of international co-operation and understanding. More would do so if they knew about such schemes.

If, instead of compelling or encouraging young men and women to spend some of the best years of their life training for war, an enlightened government offered organized opportunities for international voluntary service for peace on a really big scale to young people, it would cost far less than our military preparations cost now and the reward, in terms of international education and reconciliation, could be beyond price. In time of flood or national calamity in our own country it takes very little propaganda for a wave of practical sympathy to spread over the country so that thousands of people offer not only financial help but personal service. The goodwill is there. It needs stimulating and marshalling.

But if our organs of mass information can be so imaginatively used in time of national sorrow and need, they could, if we wished, be used also to tell us something of the need in other countries and the ways in which we could help. It can be done. And it has been done. But it will only be done as an alternative to war expenditure if all those who think that it should be, say so, and help form the public opinion to bring it about.

One of the greatest obstacles to any major change in national or world thinking is the defeatist idea that nothing we can do will make much difference. The Rector of the Imperial College of Science said a short time ago that 'any man can throw a log on the fire, but to put a billet of enriched uranium into a nuclear fire requires a long line of physicists, chemists and engineers'. Such a line has been formed because a few people believed that it could and should be done and succeeded in persuading others.

A transformation in our treatment of mental illness and of criminals came about when a few other people believed that it could and should be done and succeeded in demonstrating the possibility. National and international thinking does change. The border clashes between the Israelis and the Arabs that have occurred with such distressing regularity in recent years were once common on the border between England and Scotland. A few years ago any delegation that visited the Soviet Union was suspected to be slightly pink if not bright red. Now the Royal Society sends a delegation of scientists, and no-one is even surprised. Gallows do not ornament our cross-roads as once they did. Women are trained as doctors and engineers. At one time it was hardly thought worthwhile even to educate a girl.

All this was not the result of conscious planning by the Government; although it might have been, had there been statesmen of sufficient vision. It was the result of a gradual change of the climate of public opinion brought about by inspired and concerned men and women. A similar change could be brought about now. It is not enough only to take no personal part in war, although that is essential if conscience dictates such action. What is even more necessary is the deliberate building-up of an abhorrence of war as an evil thing. And with this there must be a sympathy for our fellowmen that seeks their well-being even to the point of personal and national sacrifice at least as great as that so gladly undertaken in wartime.

But eventually deliberate planning for a world *without* war will be as necessary at Governmental level as planning *for* war has been in the past. Any function that involves people, such as education, transport, public health, must be thought out on a national or international scale. Planning for co-operation now has so many precedents that if the will to plan internationally for peace were there, the mechanisms would not be far to seek. And the will that is required is that of ourselves, the ordinary people of the world, expressed urgently enough for those who govern not to be able to ignore it, even if they would.

CHAPTER 15

I have tried to face the political facts. As I see it, this world is doomed unless it abandons war even as a means of enforcing peaceful co-operation and other forms of good national and international behaviour. Still more if it attempts to use war as a pseudo-legal means of preventing inevitable adjustments of populations and of standards of living.

The attempt to combine gradual and agreed disarmament with a continuance of power politics has not succeeded and, it seems to me, might have been expected not to succeed.

What should now be faced is the fact that new ways of dealing both with old conflicts and with new situations must be urgently sought, and that these new forms of action will involve new thinking.

People do not generally like to think in new ways. Yet change does come. Immense changes have come, not merely in my lifetime but even within the past few years. Some of these are due to scientific advance. Others have been due to the inspiration of men and women who have initiated change from within the community: natural leaders who have formed the public opinion that changes government policies. Others again seem to have been the consequence of a public opinion that has emerged without any obviously inspired leadership, because the time was ripe for it.

There are, I believe, a great many people who long for some way of abolishing war that does not involve acquiescence in other forms of wrongdoing, or cowardly submission to greed, selfishness, blackmail, or lawlessness. They distrust their own power of being able to resist these evils in a non-violent way and so cannot: visualize a world in which non-violence has eliminated violence. Their doubts are reasonable ones. Yet the alternative is plain: disaster.

What needs building up, therefore, by every legitimate means possible (and by legitimate I now mean morally sound) is the power of individuals to be able to resist community evil of whatever kind, non-violently. Perhaps the first thing to be realized is that, while a few people may be able to do this naturally, for most it will involve not only self-discipline but a training no less arduous than that required for war. And the earlier this can be done the better. The greatness of Gandhi consisted not only in the spirit in which he himself practised non-violent resistance, but the fact that he could inspire quite ordinary men and women to do the same, although not without occasional failure and inconsistency on their part.

The second thing to be realized is that it is the resistance that matters more than the effect of the resistance. By this I mean exactly what I say. That non-violent resistance can no more guarantee a short-term victory over evil than violent resistance can; but that evil must be resisted, victory or no victory.

The third thing to be realized is that non-violent resistance to community wrongdoing is never undemocratic. Democracy is government by discussion, not government by a majority. Many dictatorships do have the support of a majority of the people, but they are bad if they eliminate or suppress the rights of the minority opposition. Democracies recognize the right to strike; and although this right may be abused, it may also very properly be exercised. If, for example, a democratically elected but reactionary government, temporarily in power, set the clock back by ordering a 12-hour working day and the industrial employment of all children over ten years of age not in fee-paying schools, there would be a sense of public outrage which would culminate in widespread civil disobedience. It would be felt that the new law was so unjust that to operate it until the time came round for another General Election would be intolerable. Similarly, a declaration of war, or the violent attack of any nation or part of a community by another, even if it were ordered by a democratically-elected government, ought to be stopped not only by non-violent resistance on the part of those attacked, but also by widespread civil disobedience on the part of those ordered to attack, because such an order should cause a sense of moral and intellectual outrage.

We need to think far more clearly about the obligations of citizenship, and to realize that any form of government is a mechanism and not a master.

The technique of non-violent resistance would be the only one that was consistent with total disarmament, and it therefore merits the most careful study by any community that even wishes to eliminate war from the world, and yet to retain justice.

As with any other technique, however, a theoretical or historical study is not enough. These are valuable, because they provide a background. But the proper way of studying the method of non-violence is to practise it, and even to experiment with it, personally.

Many Christians who are not pacifists insist that it is possible to fight and to kill without hatred, so that the teaching of Christ 'Love your enemies' can, they say, be obeyed even in wartime. I find this difficult to believe. There can be no doubt that some Christians do believe it. Whether or not love for the enemy can be felt while you are violently attacking or resisting him, however, the method of non-violence demands it. *Evil* must be resisted, non-violently but absolutely, as much for the sake of the evildoer as for the prevention of the wrong he attempts. Those who do wrong are harming themselves and need saving, rescuing if you like, from the evil that they practise or contemplate. They are men and women who are capable of goodness; and the method of non-violence seeks to turn them from evildoing to welldoing. 'Force may subdue, but love gains.'

That is also the aim of any enlightened penal system; and we have gradually been realizing more and more, since the days of Elizabeth Fry and John Howard, that its success in changing the criminal, and not just in punishing or deterring him, depends as much on those who work the system as on the system itself – or even perhaps more so. They must be people who are able to believe in the men and women among whom they work; and who want to reclaim them for society because they do believe in them.

Only the exceptional person, however, is able to feel a deep affection for, and interest in, the misfit and the criminal; and so it is best to begin with those whom we ordinary people love naturally. When we begin there, we begin to realize that practical forms of non-violent living, and even of non-violent resistance to evil, are part of our everyday experience. Every time we have given the 'soft answer' that 'turneth away wrath' we have practised the technique of non-violence. It is a common experience that it takes two to make a quarrel. When two bad-tempered people live together without making any effort at self-control, even though they are fond of each other, life can be hell for those around them. But if one deliberately holds back the sharp answer he would like to give, he makes it easier for tempers to subside and even, perhaps, for an apology to follow.

Of course the soft answer must be given in affection and not from cowardice, still less because it is intended to be deliberately provoking! It is just here that the underlying attitude of real love towards the offender, with its intuitive knowledge of what is most required, needs emphasis. Cowardice, or the attitude of 'anything for a quiet life', may very well encourage an insolent or bullying spirit. Silent contempt can be more violent than a blow. Contempt has no place at all in the method of non-violence. Jesus Christ made this clear when He said 'Ye have heard that it was said by them of old time, "Thou shalt not kill: and whosoever shall kill shall be in danger of the judgment"; but I say unto you, "That . . . whosoever shall say 'Thou fool', shall be in danger of hell fire".' We injure ourselves by the feeling of contempt as much as we injure others.

If someone we love does have a bad temper, we try to avoid the circumstances that provoke it. If it is so easily provoked that we cannot avoid it, the soft answer may have to include, then or later, a quiet but firm reproof, for their own sake as well as ours. But very often our ability to co-operate peacefully with our family, our neighbours, and our fellow-workers does depend upon our knowing how, with courtesy, to refuse to be drawn into particular types of discussion or to take sides on questions which arouse needless passions. We may do this in particular when we know that they have violent prejudices which we do not share, but which we are not likely to be able to remove by argument. Or when the dispute is about a matter of fact that could easily be determined by experiment or by consulting a work of reference.

All these are the small changes of everyday life, but they count for happiness in living together as persons, and they are a pointer to happiness in living together as nations. It seems to me that rather than thinking first in terms of resistance, even of non-violent resistance, we should think first of learning how to live and work together, without self-assertion, without selfishness, without constant recrimination and bitterness, not expecting one another to cheat, to rob, or to murder. Knowing our own weaknesses, we must sometimes deliberately tolerate and make allowances for the weaknesses of others. We do not need to be looking at each other all the time, seeking for something to practise nonviolent resistance against!

We have to recognize also that from some points of view other nations may be passing through the stage of historical adolescence and need special understanding. When we live with children we do not expect them to behave as adults. But neither, if we have any sense, do we insist that we have all wisdom and all knowledge and never make any mistakes ourselves. Our first and most essential form of non-violent resistance must be to the temptation to think that we have nothing to learn from others, or that co-operation is impossible unless they do as we say and not as we do.

We do in fact co-operate, as individuals and as nations, with people whose politics, religion, and habits are quite different from our own, even with those whose values are different from ours. Mohammedans and Christians have joined together in the Baghdad Pact. The USA and Yugoslavia are friendly in spite of their respective capitalist and communist economies. Spain has still a Falangist government, yet Soviet scientists came to Madrid during Holy Week, 1956, to attend a scientific conference. I met them there; and they even spent a holiday touring the South of Spain when the conference was over, with the consent of the authorities on both sides. This is plain common sense, because a free interchange of scientific knowledge benefits everyone. But so does all free co-operation.

And just as on a personal level we try to be accommodating, so we must try to understand each other at a national level. We can learn not to irritate or be irritated by the fact that we have different standards and habits in our

attitudes to punctuality, to cleanliness, to courtesy, to work, to religious ob-
servance, or to police courts. Of course we may try to educate one another
if we can do it in a non-offensive way; but above all, we must learn to laugh
together, even though our sense of humour may be different. The late Dame
Lilian Barker, former Governor of the Aylesbury Borstal Institution for
Girls, said that she had laughed more people into being good than if she had
preached for hours. Laughing with people is very different from laughing
at them.

None of this is really soul-shaking. It is the daily drill of the barrack
square. If it is not easy to keep it up, it becomes easier with practise. What is
much more difficult is resistance to group pressures to wrong social action,
especially if the pressure comes from those who are our friends. We do not
want to seem Pharisaical nor to appear to sit in judgement on our friends,
but resistance to evil must include resistance to the evil in our own society
before we can hope to be able to resist evils imposed on us. Quite apart from
military preparations and military adventures, there are other community
evils to resist. There is the pressure to sexual licence, or to excessive drinking
or gambling. As a nation we spent £859 million on alcoholic drinks in 1955
and £880 million on smoking, more than thirty times as much as we did on
all forms of international organization.

It is not easy to resist bureaucratic inhumanity. Yet as planning increases
– and it must increase if all sections of the world community are to be ad-
equately fed – there is a tendency to sacrifice individuals who get in the way,
or who are awkward and refuse to conform. They are quietly offered up on
the altar to efficiency. Publicity is helpful in preventing this, but it needs
someone to sound the alert. Sectional selfishness is another evil that needs
watching in our own community, especially as it can disguise itself as group
self-respect or family responsibility.

It is possible to oppose wrongdoing in our own community, in our own
section of the community, only by continual individual vigilance, and by a
steadfast determination neither to condone, nor to ignore, nor to participate in
wrongdoing, no matter what the consequences to ourselves may be, no matter

if we seem to stand absolutely alone. We are not free, even in our own country, from interference with civil liberties. These are too precious to allow them to be lost in the interests of political convenience. We can see the dangers when we look at other countries where racial discrimination, religious persecution, State interference with intellectual integrity, or the imposition of loyalty oaths and other forms of thought control have become major problems.

Many reasonable and thoughtful people in Germany have now realized that the mistake they made in the early 1930s, and for which the whole world paid dearly, was not to have opposed the rising tide of Hitlerism *as individuals,* no matter what the immediate consequences to themselves or even to their families. The path of dictators and of demagogues is greatly eased by the reluctance of men and women to resist as individuals, because it seems politically futile to do so. In *Speak Truth to Power*,[21] American Friends recall the history of Thomas Garrett, a Delaware Quaker who was convicted and fined for his activities on the 'underground railroad' by means of which slaves made their way to freedom. The fine was so heavy that it left him financially ruined, yet Thomas Garrett stood up in Court and said

> Judge, thou has left me not a dollar, but I wish to say to thee and to all in this courtroom that if anyone knows a fugitive who wants a shelter and a friend, send him to Thomas Garrett and he will befriend him.

Defiance? Yes, of course, but it is such defiance that changes history.

Coming nearer to our own day, I happened to be in Gottingen in July 1955 a few weeks after the Rector of the University had resigned in protest against the appointment of a neo-Nazi as local Minister of Education. He felt that he must do so, since other forms of protest had been ineffective. He then found that he was supported, not only by his own academic staff, but by a considerable weight of world opinion, so much so that the Minister in ques-

21 American Friends Service Committee, 20 S. 12th Street, Philadelphia 7, Pa, USA. Available also from Friends Book Centre, Euston Road, London, NW 1, England.

tion was obliged to resign. This kind of action is not easy for the individual, perhaps it is even more difficult than the nonviolent opposing of an alien and imposed government, but there are many such 'victories without violence' in history, some brought about by individuals, others by groups of individuals. Nevertheless they are less well known than military victories.

If we wish to encourage young people to be able to stand alone, if need be, against governmental or group wrongdoing, they should hear much more in the course of their education about bravery, courage, and sacrifice of this kind and its inevitable place in future history. One of the difficulties of education for a peaceful world is that it seems so tame. In actual fact I believe that so far from being tame, the intellectual and moral effort required to build up the national character to the point where wrongdoing and injustice can be opposed firmly, steadfastly, constructively, and without violence, will be greater than any effort that we have yet been called upon to attempt. And it is one in which if they would, the Churches could co-operate most effectively. Refusal to take part in evil, and redemption by sacrificial love are basic to the Christian faith.

Let me be more specific. Suppose we were disarmed, and a nation which had either not disarmed at all, or which had secretly rearmed, were to invade us. Could we resist? Perhaps the first question to ask is 'Ought we to resist?' We do not admit the right of Cypriots forcibly to resist our government of their island, although we hold it only for strategic purposes. Would we admit their right to resist us non-violently by civil disobedience and similar methods? Do we admit the right of the 70,000 or more negroes, 'second-class citizens' of Montgomery, Alabama, to boycott the buses on which members of their race were being insulted? Every week their young Christian leader, Dr Martin Luther King, would lead his fellow-Negroes in several hours of prayer and of training in the technique of non-violence: 'We are not against the white people. We do not wish to put the bus company out of business but to put justice into the bus company.' Is that right?

When I mentioned, earlier in this chapter, the reclaiming of a criminal by enlightened methods of penal reform, I was speaking of a criminal who was in our power, who had been caught and convicted. But now we are thinking of an occasion when we may be in the power of someone else, and that someone else an invader. The fact that he has used force against us has put him in the wrong. But we may have injured him first in some other way. We may, in the past, have taken his raw materials at an uneconomic price. We may have governed him harshly or treated him contemptuously and left a bitter scar. We may be trying to hold on to a standard of living which is so much higher than his that the temptation to invade and to force us to share is a compelling one. We should be clear that we are not also in the wrong.

If the method of non-violent resistance is to be used it must be used with discrimination against *evil*, and not merely for its nuisance value, and it must make a positive appeal to the good side of the enemy. If orders were issued which were good in themselves, that schools should remain open, for example, and that teachers should continue to teach, there could be no ground for civil disobedience even though the order came from an alien government. But if teachers were ordered to teach wrong ideas they should refuse at once, and be able to explain, why they did so. If some teachers collaborated with the invader (as happened in Norway for example, during the Nazi invasion) and did teach wrong ideas, every effort should be made to dissuade them from doing so. Moreover, the children themselves should be encouraged to resist evil ideas and to boycott the classes in which they were taught.

This would almost inevitably bring reprisals. One of the most difficult consequences of resistance to evil is that it may entail not only suffering for oneself, prison, torture, or perhaps even death, but also similar suffering for one's family. Yet here again, why should the man who resists evil peaceably but absolutely expect to escape more lightly than the military man? The nation, when it goes into war, knows that it will sacrifice thousands, or in a future war even millions of families. Gone forever are the days when a soldier could imagine that if he were risking his life, at least his family would be safe.

What is essential in the future is that every member of the family, even little children, should learn at whatever cost not to give way to wrong or to co-operate in it. That this can be done was proved long since in the history of the Society of Friends, when every adult Friend in certain districts being imprisoned for worshipping as they thought right, the children in those areas continued to meet for worship, in their meetinghouses, as their parents had done.

It would mean also that if another nation was invaded, and not our own, the support that we could give them would be limited to moral support. That is so very often to-day. It will in any case be so in the future unless we intend to destroy the world to prevent aggression. But moral support is powerful in proportion to the integrity of the nation that gives it.

It is not possible to give a blueprint for what action would actually be taken against an invader by a nation trained not to co-operate with evil. It was not surprising to learn that Hitler had proposed, when he had successfully invaded Britain, to suppress all pacifist organizations, including the Society of Friends. He would not have succeeded in doing so even if he had murdered the lot, for if there is one thing that is certain, it is that ideas cannot be suppressed. I simply do not believe that men can be so conditioned that evil triumphs permanently.

What is perhaps a greater danger is that the technique of nonviolent resistance should be found to be so effective in practise that its moral content should be lost. It might then become a tool, as strikes and lockouts have sometimes become tools, for forcing sectional interests that are neither reasonable nor just.

I do not know of any way of avoiding this except by renewed vigilance, and an emphasis on the necessity, when the training of young people is involved, for making it clear that a life of nonviolence is essentially one of deep spiritual out-reach to the good in other men and of belief that, even if there is no response, even if we appear to fail, goodness will in the end prevail.

> *Yea, though I walk through the valley of the shadow of death*
> *I shall fear no evil, for Thou art with me.*